T0277219

EVERYDAY SACRED,
EVERYWHERE BEAUTY

EVERYDAY SACRED, EVERYWHERE BEAUTY

Readings from an Old Monk's Journal

ᛣ

Mary Lou Kownacki

Edited by Anne McCarthy, Linda Romey,
Jacqueline Sanchez-Small, and Katie Gordon

ORBIS BOOKS
Maryknoll, New York 10545

Founded in 1970, Orbis Books endeavors to publish works that enlighten the mind, nourish the spirit, and challenge the conscience. The publishing arm of the Maryknoll Fathers and Brothers, Orbis seeks to explore the global dimensions of the Christian faith and mission, to invite dialogue with diverse cultures and religious traditions, and to serve the cause of reconciliation and peace. The books published reflect the views of their authors and do not represent the official position of the Maryknoll Society. To learn more about Maryknoll and Orbis Books, please visit our website at www.orbisbooks.com.

Manufactured in the United States of America.
Manuscript editing and typesetting by Joan Weber Laflamme.

Library of Congress Cataloging-in-Publication Data

Names: Kownacki, Mary Lou, author.
Title: Everyday sacred, everywhere beauty : readings from an old Monk's journal / Mary Lou Kownacki ; edited by Anne McCarthy [and three others].
Description: Maryknoll, NY: Orbis Books, 2024.
Identifiers: LCCN 2024010884 (print) | LCCN 2024010885 (ebook) | ISBN 9781626985889 (trade paperback) | ISBN 9798888660454 (epub)
Subjects: LCSH: Reconciliation—Religious aspects—Christianity. | Peace. | Spiritual life. | Christian life.
Classification: LCC BT738.27 .K67 2024 (print) | LCC BT738.27 (ebook) | DDC 234/.5—dc23/eng/20240417
LC record available at https://lccn.loc.gov/2024010884
LC ebook record available at https://lccn.loc.gov/2024010885

Contents

Introduction   7

CR

Part One
SAVED BY LOVE
Journal Entries, 2011–2013
11–66

CR

Part Two
THIS I BELIEVE
Journal Entries, 2013–2019
67–148

CR

Part Three
HOLD FAST TO BEAUTY
Journal Entries, 2019–2022
149–200

CR

Afterword by Joan Chittister, OSB   201

Sources   205

Introduction

Mary Lou Kownacki, OSB, rarely made it through the day without someone turning to her for advice. Her Benedictine sisters stopped her after liturgy for a quick chat. Activists who knew her as the mother of the spirituality of nonviolence called her. Young people she had helped to raise turned up at her door. Donors to the ministries that she established, hungry neighborhood children, friends from her schooldays, waitresses from her favorite restaurants—if people crossed Mary Lou's path once, they usually came back to her, knowing that she would listen to what was on their mind and respond in a completely unpredictable, unpretentious way.

Mary Lou brought the same gusto for life and the same personal touch to thousands of devoted readers through her blogs on the website for Monasteries of the Heart. She was a cofounder, with Sister Joan Chittister, and executive director of this contemporary online monastic community, which she envisioned as a means of sharing ancient Benedictine spirituality with the modern world. For more than ten years her blogs, "Heart of the Matter" and "Old Monk's Journal," were highlights of the website, alongside resources encouraging members to get involved in good works, pray daily, form community, and practice *lectio divina*—a contemplative prayer form of spiritual reading.

This book comprises the best of those blog posts, which Mary Lou called journal entries, in which she shares childhood stories, favorite poetry, heartache, and inspiration for the darkest times with the wisdom and depth of a woman in her seventies and eighties whose entire adult life was spent as a monastic.

Born and raised in Erie, Pennsylvania, she attended St. Benedict Academy, run by the Benedictine Sisters of Erie. Shortly after graduation, at the age of seventeen, she entered the monastic community. From that time on she trained in the ancient spiritual practices found in the Rule of Saint Benedict. Figures like Thomas Merton, Daniel Berrigan, the four American churchwomen martyred in El Salvador, and Dorothy Day captured her imagination and provided a vision of what it meant to practice gospel living in a way that seriously engaged the questions and the suffering of the present day.

She was faithful to the monastic practices of *lectio divina*, conversion of life, hospitality, and peace, and she applied them to the realities of daily life with freshness and creativity, confident that the wisdom of monastic spirituality was relevant to contemporary life and ought to be broadly available to anyone who would benefit from it.

With the support of her Benedictine community, Mary Lou was instrumental in establishing many of its good works: the Pax Center, a Christian community for nonviolence that brought together sisters, activists, and the disenfranchised in a living group; a soup kitchen that eventually became Emmaus Ministries and grew to include a food pantry and an urban farm; the Inner-City Neighborhood Art House, an after-school and summer program where inner-city children receive free lessons in the visual, literary, performing, and environmental arts; and Benedictines for Peace, an organization that empowers monastics to address matters of social justice. A lifelong friend and collaborator of Erie Benedictine Joan Chittister, Mary Lou founded and served until her death as director of Benetvision, a publishing ministry that promotes Sister Joan's writing and teaching.

As much as she was perpetually innovative, Mary Lou also took seriously her position as a holder of the monastic tradition. Her Benedictine formation was heavily influenced by the Second Vatican

Council's instruction that religious communities return to their roots and the inspiration of their founders; in the case of Benedictines, this meant an emphasis on exploring the meaning and implications of a truly monastic identity. She spent her entire monastic life grappling with what it meant to be a monk and how a monk ought to engage with the modern world and the modern church. She shared on her blog the answers that emerged over the years:

> "A monk stands as a question mark to society."
> "Monasticism is a rhythm of life that fosters
>   mindfulness."
> "Monasteries are resistance centers."
> "Monasticism is a force for life."

After having written her "Heart of the Matter" blog for a number of years, Mary Lou began writing in the voice of an alter ego that she called Old Monk. While her earlier blog entries featured poetry and selections from her current reading and the conversations that filled her day-to-day life, the 2013 "Old Monk's Journal" slightly shifted the tone of her writing.

Old Monk had clearly embraced and assimilated all the ideas about monasticism, and it showed through her stories and her opinions. Old Monk, of course, was Mary Lou—they shared the same history, the same irritations, hopes, and joie de vivre—but Old Monk had an additional level of freedom: freedom to claim her authority as a seasoned monastic practitioner, freedom to rail against injustice, and freedom to be swept up in moments of worship.

This showed up in different ways in her writing. Take, for example, these words Mary Lou wrote:

> The truth is, I am not very good at listening to nature. . . .
> Before I die, I want to change. I want to connect with the
> spiders, tree limbs, stars, moon phases, and mud. In fact, Old

Monk is going out in the rain right now without an umbrella. She is going to sit in a chair in the yard and get soaking wet. And she's going to listen.

This voice, this persona, this willingness to publicly claim the tension between who she really was and who she really hoped to become, is part of what made her so beloved by her many readers at Monasteries of the Heart. That kind of honesty and hope make spiritual growth possible, for her and for other seekers.

In this book selections from her blog posts—"Heart of the Matter" and "Old Monk's Journal"—are gathered into one collection. They chronicle a wise, outrageous woman's insights into her professional and spiritual life, the turmoil of the 2016 and 2020 elections, the evolution of monastic life in an often-oppressive church, and ultimately, her own mortality and desire to live fully while undergoing treatment for a rare and aggressive cancer. Her stories and commentaries offer material for *lectio divina* that will last a lifetime.

—JACQUELINE SANCHEZ-SMALL, OSB

Part One

SAVED BY LOVE

Journal Entries, 2011–2013

☙

A Global Heart

My favorite story of Saint Benedict happened at the end of his life. According to his biographer, Gregory the Great, Benedict was standing before his window in the dead of night, wrapped in prayer. Suddenly a flood of light shone down from above, clearing away every trace of darkness. Gregory writes that according to Benedict's own description, the whole world gathered up before his eyes in what appeared to be a single ray of light.

I thought of this story while I was viewing a preview of *Globalized Soul*. There's no doubt that the filmmakers have the same vision as Benedict and know it to be the essential insight of all religion: darkness will be destroyed only when, in the light of love, we see every man and woman, every nation and culture, as one.

We are introduced in the film to many ordinary, deeply spiritual individuals, people who are devoting their lives to bringing about this oneness. We find them in dangerous and divided places, working nonviolently to make possible the dawn of a global village.

The video took three years to film and involved trips to five continents, one hundred hours of footage, and thirty-five interviews of visionary and spiritual activists representing the world's religions. It showcases sacred music and rituals from around the globe.

I have to say that I really enjoyed the sacred music, especially the Turkish Whirling Dervishes, and wished the film had given music equal time to the speakers. I think we still put too much trust in the word, rather than in music and art, to change the human heart. I say this even though Erie Benedictine Sister Joan Chittister is one of the speakers in the film, as well as His Holiness the Dalai Lama, Rabbi Michael Lerner, and Roshi Joan Halifax, among other inspirational figures.

I also like to think that this prayer, which I wrote a few years ago, is in the spirit of Benedict's vision and the *Globalized Soul*. I offer it for your consideration:

> I bow to the one who signs the cross.
> I bow to the one who sits with the Buddha.
> I bow to the one who wails at the wall.
> I bow to the OM flowing in the Ganges.
> I bow to the one facing Mecca,
> whose forehead touches holy ground.
> I bow to dervishes whirling in mystical wind.
> I bow
> to the north
> to the south
> to the east
> to the west
> I bow to the God within each heart.
> I bow to epiphany, to God's face revealed.
> I bow. I bow. I bow.

CR

A Good Laugh

A friend in California sent a photo to show us that Lucy, her newborn granddaughter, is the youngest member of Monasteries of the Heart and perfectly at home with an online community. All of us got a kick out of it.

Sometimes people worry about whether they are doing Monasteries of the Heart "right." We get occasional notes asking if there is a step-by-step program to follow to become an authentic monastic. Unfortunately, there is no such check-off list in the Rule of Saint Benedict. The Benedictine path to holiness is a way of life, just learning to live an ordinary life extraordinarily well.

And life provides ample hints at the holy. The picture of Lucy appearing on my computer screen, for example, reminded me of the importance of laughter.

At one of our community meetings the facilitator had us pair off with another sister, sit face to face, and begin laughing aloud. And continue laughing aloud. And continue. We did it for three minutes. She recommended trying it for ten minutes.

Sometimes when I'm by myself in the house I start laughing aloud—hearty and hilarious. I love it. I feel so great when I'm through—refreshed, relaxed, and content.

I also read in Oprah's magazine that one secret to a long life is to smile at yourself in the mirror when you get up in the morning. I don't know whether the practice teaches you to take yourself lightly—that your morning face, and by extension you, are a hoot, or if the smile changes your attitude toward the new day. Whatever, I am trying it.

Thank you, Lucy, for providing a good laugh. It is an essential spiritual practice of a monastery of the heart.

CR

Morning Coffee

I was part of a group of sisters that met monthly to discuss spiritual stuff. I remember one meeting when we were having a deep discussion on the meaning of life and someone asked, "Why do you get out of bed in the morning?" We started around the circle, and it was the second or third person that said, "What gets me out of bed in the morning is the thought of my first cup of coffee." We laughed. Then another sister said, "Me, too, especially if I remembered to set the timer the night before and can smell it already brewing." Then a third. A fourth. Until three-fourths of the sisters gathered admitted they got out of bed in the morning for the taste of fresh coffee.

That discussion prompted a poem in me:

> No light yet. Old Monk pours
> steaming hot coffee in a mug and sits.
> Same ritual, morning after morning—the years
>   a blur.
> "If upon awakening
> your first thought is of God,
> you are a monk," Wayne Teasdale wrote.
> What if your first thought is of coffee?
> What does that make Old Monk?
> "A lover of pleasure"
> would do as an epitaph.

Then I read this reflection by Brother David Steindl-Rast and everything fell into place:

What is it you tend to tackle with spontaneous mindfulness,
so that without an effort your whole heart is into it? Maybe

it's that first cup of coffee in the morning, the way it warms
you and wakes you up, or taking your dog for a walk, or giving a little child a piggyback ride. Your heart is in it—and so
you find meaning in it—not a meaning you could spell out
in words, but a meaning in which you can rest. These are
moments of intense prayerfulness, though we may never have
thought of them as prayer. They show us the close connection
between praying and playing. These moments when our heart
finds ever so briefly rest in God are samples that give us a taste
of what prayer is meant to be. If we could maintain this inner
attitude, our whole life would become prayer.

ᘓ

On Retreat

I'm on retreat this week. As in the past fifty-two years, I'm participating in the annual retreat of the Benedictine Sisters of Erie.
I always look forward to the week for a chance to rest, receive new
insights, reflect, and renew my spirit.

And yet, when I look back over these five decades, there are few
retreat leaders whose names I even remember, let alone recall what
they said. So, are retreats all they're cracked up to be?

I was a novice, only eighteen years old, when I attended a retreat
led by Father Kieran, a young Benedictine monk from Latrobe,
Pennsylvania. Father Kieran drew on mystical writings and wove
poetry, music, and art into his conferences. He made my head swim
with a God of beauty and mystery, even though I had absolutely
no idea what he was talking about. His God was way beyond the
imagination, let alone the experiences, of this teenager who still
equated holiness with devotions, rules, and rituals. But he sparked
a flame inside me that never died—I wanted to know the God
that he knew.

James Finley, noted author and retreat director, came bearing incense and prayer gongs and Eastern mystique. What I remember about Finley is that he freed me to pray.

I identified with Finley because, like myself, he was a prayer-method addict. In search of the "perfect" prayer, both of us had tried yoga, chanting, centering prayer, meditation. Finally, Finley was told by his spiritual director to trust the prayer method that God had given him—writing. Finley told us that he prayed best by writing. Well, so did I. And it was good.

Next, I remember the Native American Sister José Hobday, a mountain of a woman in stature, style, and spirit. In solidarity with the world's poor, she owned only one dress. She had us throw coins in the air during a conference to practice detachment. She invited us to dance with her in a thunderstorm under the stars. As part of her retreat, each of us gave to the poor an item we didn't need, one we loved, and something that was deeply precious to us. She was wild and audacious in her interpretations of living the gospel. How I envied and lusted to be that free in the arms of God.

And finally, there was Edwina Gateley. I sobbed through most of her retreat. Gateley, a poet and international speaker, started homes for prostitutes and street people in Chicago. Like Jesus, she told us story upon story of broken lives and the tender mercy of God. She gave vivid accounts of going into the toughest bars of Chicago, listening to street women, and accepting them without judgment. If you're lucky, at least once in your life you will meet the compassionate heart of God. Gateley was that for me.

So, are retreats worth it? I think so. The four I vividly remember focused my spiritual path. One gave me an unquenchable thirst for the divine. The second centered me in my particular path to God. The third made me roll the dice for freedom of spirit as the only virtue worth dying for. And the last enforced the spiritual truth that all this prayer, all this retreat stuff is straw and chaff unless we grow into the compassionate heart of God.

CR

Father's Day Gift

How do you celebrate Father's Day if your dad is dead? I suppose you do a lot of remembering. "One good memory may be the means of saving us," Dostoyevsky wrote. I'm one of the lucky ones. I have a thousand good memories of my father.

I'm one of those daughters—for better or worse—whose father became a mythical hero figure. Who is the best teacher I ever had? My brilliant father. Who is the face of God for me? My father of unconditional love. What centered me in an ocean of trust and gave me the security to risk almost anything life offered? The memory of being a child listening to nightly bedtime stories wrapped lovingly in my father's massive, Herculean-like arms.

You get the idea. Like I said, for better or worse.

But what I want to remember this Father's Day is my father's love of song. My dad had a rich, tenor voice. And he sang at every opportunity. I remember him singing with Mario Lanza's recordings and later in life with Pavarotti and Bocelli CDs. He spent many hours in his favorite chair singing his favorite hymns aloud. He led the church choir for forty years and was an invited soloist at weddings; funerals; and civic, religious, and ethnic celebrations. He sang with the family on Sunday afternoon drives and with the neighborhood kids on car trips to the beach.

When I was a difficult infant, he walked me night after night, rocking me in his massive arms and singing "Let Me Call You Sweetheart" until I fell asleep. As a child, I would get a dollar for listening to his favorite records, memorizing the words, and writing them out for him. I still remember most of "Bluebird of Happiness." The strongest memory I have of my mother's funeral is of my dad walking down the aisle ahead of the casket, his voice breaking with grief, yet filling the church with the most revered of Polish hymns, "*Serdeczna Matko.*"

Not that our relationship was a perfect "ten." Once I became a teenager, I rebelled in just about every facet of our relationship. Even his singing became an irritation. And at public gatherings—because it drew attention—his singing became an embarrassment. But thank God everyone grows up.

Now, I sit in my favorite chair and listen to all his favorite recordings. And I love them. What better way to keep my father's memory alive?

ભ

On Silence

A college student spent a couple of weeks at the Erie Benedictine monastery doing research for a paper on feminist models of leadership. I was one of the sisters that she interviewed, and during our conversation I asked how her monastery experience was going.

"I wasn't prepared for the personal spiritual impact," she said, explaining it was the silence that forced her to do some intense soul searching. She went on to explain that in all her twenty or so years of life she had never experienced this kind of silence, especially recently—no headphones every waking hour, no TV blaring as background, no din and shouting, no constant dorm chatter. "It's so different," she said. "The silence forced me to look into myself and do a lot of spiritual searching."

The conversation reminded me of an article I read in a recent *The Sun* magazine. The article was an interview with Gordon Hempton, an acoustic ecologist, who travels the globe recording the sounds of nature—birdsong, crashing waves, rain drops on a rainforest floor—vanishing because of the intrusion of human activity. Hempton's research shows that the average daytime noise-free interval in our wilderness areas and national parks is now less than five minutes.

His campaign is to get the government to legislate for "One Square Inch of Silence" in our national parks. Specifically, he is working to establish a twenty-mile-radius no-flight zone over Olympic National Park in Washington State. This space would be totally free of human noise, including the banning of overhead planes except for search-and-rescue missions and medical evacuations. He said in the interview, "What if we were to maintain absolute silence at a single point—one square inch of the planet earth? The result would mean managing or limiting noise pollution for an area of about a thousand square miles."

Isn't "One Square Inch of Silence" an interesting and imaginative idea? It got me thinking of a variation on the theme. How about one hour of silence in my day, or one room for silence in my home, or one day of silence in my month? What would be the result of all those single points of silence?

"Listen" is the first word in the Rule of Saint Benedict. It's been my experience that the person you need to listen to first and befriend is yourself. You've got to hear all the pain, the suffering, the tears, the hurt you've inflicted on others and experienced yourself. You can only do that through silence. That's the groundwork before you can really hear another's pain, before you can hear the cry of the world. Before the world can really change into the compassionate heart of God.

☙

No Matter What

"Julian of Norwich, a fourteenth-century female mystic, saw the life struggle as coming to discover that we are 'clothed in God's goodness.'" This sentence comes from a remarkable book that I just finished reading, and, in a sense, sums it up.

I've come late to the book, but thank God I found it. I'm talking about *Tattoos on the Heart* by Gregory Boyle. This has to be in the top five of the best spiritual books I've read. Boyle is a Jesuit priest and founder and executive director of Homeboy Industries, which serves eight thousand gang members from seven hundred different gangs in Los Angeles.

The book is not a written documentary on the extraordinary efforts of Homeboy Industries—a charter school, counseling, tattoo removal, job placement and training, five in-house businesses—but a kind of beatific vision. Everywhere you look in this book you see the face of God.

In chapter after chapter we meet young men and women whose lives are tsunamis of neglect, abuse, drug addiction, violence, and shame. We meet them in gang-infested neighborhoods. We meet them in the many prisons he visits. We meet them in Homeboy Industries. We meet them in failure after failure. We meet them clutching a slim ray of hope, and then being crushed by unrelenting darkness. These are tough and tragic stories, not the feel-good superficial success stories we like to feed on. But Boyle is about much more than our measurement of success. He writes:

Out of the wreck of our disfigured, misshapen selves, so darkened by shame and disgrace, indeed the Lord comes to us disguised as ourselves. And we don't grow into this—we just learn to pay better attention. The "no matter whatness" of God dissolves the toxicity of shame and fills us with tender mercy.

Boyle is about loving "no matter what." That's a tough one. Is there anyone reading this who hasn't struggled with loving "no matter what"? Loving me, no matter what? Loving you, no matter what? Loving a criminal, no matter what? Loving an enemy, no matter what?

I don't know about you, but I've heard myself say things like this: "God can't possibly love me because I. . . ." "What do I do about a drug-addicted child who is wrecking our family? Is my

unconditional love helping or harming?" "Do I draw a line when
a person who lives on the street keeps asking for help, not once,
not twice, but for twenty long years and counting?" "How many
chances are too many chances?" "How do you reconcile tough love
and God's love?"

There are no easy answers here. So, I recommend reading the
book and seeing what you think afterward. My take on it is this:
It might take a lifetime for some to discover they are "clothed
in God's goodness." Others may die without the knowledge. Or
maybe it occurs at the moment of the last breath. But as Boyle's life
attests, we take a chance on loving into loveliness. He writes, "To
that end, we choose to become what child psychiatrist Alice Miller
calls 'enlightened witnesses'—people who through their kindness,
tenderness, and focused, attentive love return folks to themselves."

That's our job: kindness, tenderness, attentive love. That's all, folks.
The end result is not ours to know or measure.

CR

Seek Beauty and Pursue It

I read this from Francis of Assisi this morning:

> Dear God, please reveal to us
> your sublime
> beauty
> that is everywhere, everywhere, everywhere
> so that we will never again
> feel frightened.

The words comforted me, and I marked the page so I could copy
them into my commonplace book. But I did wonder how beauty
takes away fear. I tried to imagine myself back in Paris at the Monet
Museum, sitting in the center of an oval room surrounded on all

sides by Monet's paintings of luscious water lilies. I guess at a deep level I did feel without fear.

Psychologist Rollo May tells us that beauty is the only human experience that gives us a sense of joy and peace simultaneously. It makes us serene while exhilarating us; it evokes wonder and time-lessness. Beauty, in other words, helps us transcend our tragedies and the fears that ensue.

That's why I'm intent, for the years I have left, to seek beauty and pursue it. I think a commitment to become aware of beauty is the most important spiritual practice I can adopt. So, I plan to spend time in nature as often as I can. I revel in flowers. I'm collecting paintings that I love and keeping them at my side. I go to museums and galleries and offbeat art shops. I try to listen to music every day. And, of course, I want to look, really look, at the face of every person I meet. To paraphrase Victor Hugo, "To love another person is to touch the face of Beauty."

I'm also going to start to pray to Beauty, as in "Our Beauty who are in heaven" and "Glory be to Beauty, and to the Christ, and to the Spirit." Maybe the practice will heighten my awareness of Beauty everywhere and erase all leftover fears.

⁂

O Happy Flaw

It happened again. The graphic artist came in distraught. "The fundraiser invitations were put in the mail this morning, and we just discovered the date is wrong." Admittedly, this is a major error, but after more than forty years of experience in publishing books, newsletters, magazines, and now blogs, I can't get too excited.

I've come to expect that almost every publication will have one flaw no matter how many times it's proofed. And I've made my peace with flaws. Especially after someone told me that one of the Native American tribes deliberately put a flaw in each piece of art they created. It was to remind them that nothing is perfect save God.

So, it's freeing to know that mistakes are part of the human condition.

Then I read this from Hopi potter Al Qöyawayma, "The flaw should not take away from the overall form, beauty, and essence of the vessel. . . . In the same way, a flaw in your own life, which often cannot be seen by others, should not keep you from reflecting your overall form and beauty."

In the case of the invitation, well, the date is wrong, but it's a beautiful piece, easily fixed with a follow-up postcard.

All of this reminded me of a birthday card that I received a few years ago and kept. It made me laugh hard and keeps all publication mistakes in perspective:

A group of monks are copying the laws of the church by hand. A new monk notices that they're copying from copies, not from the original manuscript.

He tells the head monk, "If there was an error in the first copy, every copy after that would have the same error!"

The head monk says, "Good point," and goes to get the original manuscript. Later the young monk finds the head monk with head on the desk crying, "They forgot the 'R'!!" "They forgot the 'R'!"

The young monk asks, "Father, what's wrong?" Choking back tears, the old monk replies, "The word is 'celebRate!,' 'celebRate!'"

ॐ

Find the Artichokes

I'm back at the desk after a weeklong vacation. The seven days were just enough to rest and re-energize. Now I've got to remember that even more important than extended time away are the mini-vacations we can take within the twenty-four hours we are given over and over again.

In one of my favorite books, *Haiku Mind: 108 Poems to Cultivate Awareness and Open Your Heart*, Patricia Donegan writes, "There is a word in Tibetan Buddhism, '*lungta*,' or 'windhorse,' meaning 'uplifted energy,' something primordial within every living thing, which we can tap into anytime to refresh ourselves and uplift our spirits."

She lists a few examples such as opening a window to let in fresh air, taking off your shoes before entering a room, or simply picking up your head when feeling tired. These simple actions catch the "windhorse," and the spirit sails. I don't know about you, but I have a few *lungta* in my life. For example, I like to stare out windows for a few minutes every day. I like to stand in the shower, water pouring upon me. Both of these tap into my *lungta*. I know because I've gotten some of my best ideas staring and showering. I need some time alone in the early morning. If I don't experience a touch of solitude, my day suffers. I need to write regularly; it uplifts my soul.

What perplexes me is that I know what renews me, and yet I often ignore it. I love to be by water—reading, writing, and mostly sitting. I live on a Great Lake. I haven't been there once this summer. Sometimes I quit writing for long periods of time. Instead of sitting quietly with my coffee in early morning, I often open the door for the morning paper. Then I wonder why I'm so tired, de-energized, lacking passion. I start to talk about needing a vacation. Of course, what I need is to stop ignoring *lungta* (windhorse).

If you need more proof, here's a story about Henri Matisse told by his friend, the well-known conductor Andre Kostelanetz:

When I arrived at Matisse's home, I was not only late but exhausted. The exuberant artist listened good-humoredly. "My friend," he said, "you must find the artichokes in your life!"

I was frankly baffled. Then Matisse, motioning to follow him, stepped outside. We walked through the garden until we came to the artichokes. "Every morning, after having worked for a stretch, I come here," he said, "and watch the play of light and shade on the leaves. Though I have painted over two thousand canvases, I always find new combinations of colors and fantastic patterns. No one is allowed to disturb me in this ritual of discovery; it gives me fresh inspiration, necessary relaxation, and a new perspective toward my work!"

CR

Prayer in Time of Terrorism

I wrote this prayer for Pax Christi USA, the national Catholic peace movement, ten years ago and wanted to share it again on the anniversary of 9/11.

O God, I do not know where to turn in a time of terrorism. I have no easy answers or solutions to acts of terror against the innocent. When buildings explode without warning, when the defenseless are murdered without reason, I am tempted to retaliate with vengeance. I am tempted to place the flag above the cross and put my faith in the state rather than the Sermon on the Mount. I am afraid to face my deepest fears of suffering and death, both for myself and those I love.

O God, be merciful to me a sinner and understand my weakness, my lack of trust. I lift my heart to a God of forgiveness, of compassion, of peace. I believe that You are not present in any act of violence. I believe that every human being is a child of God and that all nations and religions are embraced by You. I believe that violence ignites greater violence and that in the long line of history our only lasting legacy is love.

I recommit myself to nonviolence as a witness of Your love. I will cast out fear and boldly live love for neighbor and

enemy. I will cast out fear and renounce hatred, desire for revenge and works of war. I will cast out fear and publicly proclaim that You are a God of unlimited and unconditional love.

I recommit myself to nonviolence as a witness to Your love.
I will embrace the suffering of others and wipe every tear
from their eyes. I will devote my days to works of mercy and
justice, not to deeds of death and destruction. I will give my
passion to kindness and beauty and imagination. I commit to
hope and the children of tomorrow. Amen.

℞

Rocketman

There I was standing and clapping wildly to Elton John's "Croco-
dile Rock" and "Rocketman" and "Bennie and the Jets" and
"Goodbye Yellow Brick Road." Me and eighteen thousand other
people at the sold-out Blossom Music Center in Cleveland.

How did I get so lucky to attend the Elton John 2011 Tour? My
friend, Sister Mary Miller, had written on her bucket list: "See a
live Elton John concert." She mentioned it to someone and, voila,
free tickets.

We had a wonderful time, one of those experiences where you
leave shouting, "It's great to be alive!!!"

On the way home I started to think about my bucket list. I have
had such opportunities in life that it is hard to make a list. I've
traveled more than was in anyone's imagination when I knocked
on the door of the semi-cloistered monastery at the age of seventeen. I've prayed with the Celts on the Isle of Iona and thousands
of youth in Taizé. I've experienced the Book of Kells in Dublin
and the checkpoints and searches into Northern Ireland. I've been
to London and Paris—*ooh là là*—twice, and to Haiti five times. I
kissed the ground in Poland. I've been able to initiate a number of
projects and movements that I found meaningful. I've known deep
friendship and love. I've had my share of detractors and enemies.

I've seen great theater, attended poetry readings, participated in the great peace movement that swept our country in the 1960s and 1970s. I've known ultimate human freedom when I committed acts of civil disobedience or put my life in jeopardy by accompanying the Haitian people to the voting booth under threat of military retaliation. Suffice it to say I've had a full life.

So . . . a bucket list? It almost seems gluttonous to wish for more. I'll limit the list to four items:

- Sit in Krakow Square one more time.
- Par an eighteen-hole golf course or at least a nine-hole one.
- Finish a book I'm writing titled *God the Tavern-Keeper*
- If I'm alive when someone figures out human beings can fly, do it immediately.

If I had to limit it to one item, it would be flying. I don't like planes, but the thought of me soaring through the air—AH! If none of these happen, no big deal. After all, I got to see an Elton John concert live—and it wasn't even on my bucket list.

❦

Buddhist Training

Buddhist monks from Tibet are in Erie this week for five days. Gannon University, a local Roman Catholic institution, brought them on campus for interreligious dialogue and cultural exchange.

I went to the opening event of Buddhist chant, ritual, and dance. One of the monastic exercises the monks demonstrated for the audience was "debate." The monk emcee explained that as part of their training the monks debate spiritual teachings for three hours a day, six days a week. The debates get very physical and animated. To demonstrate, one monk sat on the stage floor and the others argued with him vehemently, challenging his every utterance, pushing and shoving, swinging their mala beads wildly over his head occasionally, until the monk came to some "enlightenment." The training for full enlightenment takes about twenty years.

As I was leaving a woman grabbed me and said, "What did you think of that, Sister?" Before I could answer, she continued, "I had to leave. I got too nervous and upset. It looked so violent. I could never do it. I would wilt and cry. There has to be another way."

I smiled and went on my way. She's right. There are other ways. But what I was thinking was, my family gatherings are Buddhist training sessions. This past Fourth of July, for example, we held the usual family-and-friends picnic that erupted into shouting debates that made the monks look like wimps. It got so animated that one person left for a smoke, three others went to another corner of the yard, many others ran inside for safety and shelter. I loved it.

All I could think of was how happy my deceased father must be, knowing the family tradition lives on without him. He was a great Master Monk, always asking provocative questions, never accepting an easy answer, forcing you to argue both sides of a question. He did it at the dinner table and at most family gatherings. These debates always meant loud, loud voices, fists slamming on tables, red faces, veins popping in the neck and when it was over—it was over.

Just like at our Fourth of July picnic when the debate focused on labor unions—a very spiritual topic, one at the heart of Catholic social teaching. When it was over the debaters shared a drink and laughed a lot. All of them had withstood the onslaught, explained, and clarified their positions, listened and—maybe even—learned a bit. One step toward enlightenment.

CR

Live in the Books You Love

I've kept a list of all the books I've read for the last thirty-seven years. Just in case you're interested, I've read 1,157 books in that time, approximately thirty-one a year. My record year is 1995, when I read fifty-two books, although I will probably surpass it this year because, thanks to a Kindle Christmas gift, I am at number forty-five and have three months to go.

Yes, I love to read. It's always a surprise, though, to leaf through the list and discover that I don't remember much of what I've read. Most of the books are a blur as to plot and characters or, in the case of nonfiction, purpose. But now and then there is a gem, a book that meets this lofty advice from Rainer Maria Rilke in *Letters to a Young Poet*:

> Live for a while in the books you love. Learn from them what is worth learning, but above all love them. This love will be returned to you a thousand times over. Whatever your life may become, these books—of this I am certain—will weave through the web of your unfolding. They will be among the strongest of all threads of your experiences, disappointments, and joys.

For example, I was asked to complete a survey recently and one of the questions was: "What is your favorite book?" Of all 1,157 books, I can still answer, *All Quiet on the Western Front* by Erich Maria Remarque. Why? Because, as Rilke noted, this book "wove itself through my unfolding."

Prior to this book, I did not question war and thought all enemies of my country were evil. Then I met Paul, the protagonist of *All Quiet*, a young German soldier fighting against my country during World War I. Surprisingly, with each turning page I found myself caring for Paul more deeply. The "enemy" had friends, a family, wanted to be a writer, loved to read . . . the "enemy" was just like me. Paul and I even shared the same favorite food—potato pancakes. When he went home on a brief furlough and his mother crawled out of her sickbed to prepare potato pancakes for her son, I thought of how my mother did the same for my brother when he came home from Vietnam. I sobbed through that scene.

After meeting Paul, the word *enemy* lost its meaning and I began to devote my life to ending war, to weaving peace and nonviolence into my life.

CR

Saved By Love

This weekend I celebrated a milestone—fifty years as a Benedictine Sister of Erie. It was a weekend of celebration with family and friends, many of whom I hadn't seen in years.

It also provided opportunity for me to look over my life and be forced to my knees in a prayer of gratitude.

When I was in high school, I wrote a short story around the parable of the Lost Sheep.

It took place in a Catholic girls' high school and the main character, a sophomore, was cleaning out her locker because she had been expelled for stealing. Alone in the hall, she realizes that the door to one of the classrooms is open. It's a religion class, and she overhears the teacher, a sister, reading the parable of the lost sheep to the students and explaining how God never gives up on anyone—that God searches out the lost and wounded, gathers them in loving arms, and all of heaven rejoices.

The young girl begins to weep.

The last line of the short story reads: "She emptied all her stuff in her school bag and slammed the locker shut, the clang echoing in the empty hall. Perhaps because of the noise, the nun teaching the religion class reached out her arm and closed the classroom door with a heavy and final thud."

Of course, when I was a sophomore, I was almost expelled from high school for shoplifting, so I had a direct inspiration for this short story.

Needless to say, the good sisters of Saint Benedict did not expel me. Like the shepherd in the parable, they sought out what was lost and led me home. The result was that at a very impressionable age I knew that I was saved by love, by unearned love, by an undeserving second chance.

It wasn't the first time. Certainly not the last. But it marked me for life.

One would hope this overflowing love tendered me, softened me, toward the lost. Or, at the very least, made me responsible for the lost—what I had been given I needed to return. One would hope. . . .

It was this memory and so many more examples of unearned love that I have experienced from the Benedictine Sisters of Erie for over fifty years that I celebrated with a deep prayer of thanksgiving.

☙

Heart of Mary

The Benedictine Sisters of Erie have a tradition of giving a "title" to each sister on the day of her final profession. For the most part the titles are given to match some virtue or aspect that is glimpsed in the sister receiving it, one she might aspire to develop further.

I never thought this worked with me. I was given the title "Of the Immaculate Heart of Mary." Actually, I was a bit embarrassed by the title and never spoke of it. I thought it too pietistic and sentimental. I would have liked "The Nonviolence of Jesus" or "The Solitude of Benedict" or "The Compassion of God." Something I could brag about.

One of the sisters in our community cross-stitched each sister's title on a very attractive banner. Many sisters hung them in their rooms. I put mine in a trunk. The banners are placed in our caskets at the time of death, and I figured someone would find mine and do the appropriate thing.

But then my 50th Jubilee came along, and I was asked to get my title banner so it could be displayed. Reluctantly, I went to the locked trunk to get it. Then a funny thing happened.

I looked at that banner and thought—Mary Lou, why have you ignored this? First, you have always had great devotion to Mary, so a Marian title is appropriate for you. Second, the title captures the essence of the monastic quest—purity of heart. Our search is to see as God sees—"Blessed are the pure (immaculate) of heart, they shall see God." Or as one of our monastic mothers, Mechthild of Magdeburg, wrote: "The day of my spiritual awakening was the day I saw all things in God and God in all things."

But third, and most important, the *Immaculate Heart of Mary* is an image of the feminine heart of God. Originally titled *The Sacred Heart of Mary*, the image depicts the flaming heart of divine love and the radiant heart of divine light. It's a heart that beats with compassionate love for all people. It's an image that I need to emulate.

Why, I asked myself, would you have a statue of Quan Yin, the Buddhist Goddess of Compassion (she who harkens to the cries of the world) on your prayer shelf and not an image of the Christian equivalent, the Sacred Heart of Mary? Why indeed?

Thank God that is now rectified. A friend gave me a beautiful depiction of the *Immaculate Heart of Mary* for my jubilee, and she and Quan Yin are now side by side.

Maybe someone did know what they were doing when they gave me the title "Of the Immaculate Heart of Mary." It just took me fifty years to figure it out.

❧

To Vow Nonviolence

A friend wrote me recently about going to a Pax Christi weekend that concluded with the group standing and reciting a vow of nonviolence. She wrote of the vow, "It's a wonderful statement of both the dreams and the challenges of nonviolence (starting with our hearts)."

Her brief note brought two warm memories to mind. One was a meeting in 1978 with Eileen Egan, Dorothy Day's good friend and a cofounder of Pax Christi USA, the national Catholic peace movement. It took place in a small restaurant that Thomas Merton used to frequent when he was a student at Columbia University. I was writing a book on nonviolence and monasticism and shared with Eileen the idea of religious taking a vow of nonviolence. This was about eight years before I became national coordinator of Pax Christi USA and was able to implement the vow for all seekers of peace. Eileen was enthusiastic about the idea as long as it included both personal and institutional violence. "Make it clear," she said, "that the vow means you do not support violence by your own nation state."

The second memory occurred in a desert at the Nevada Nuclear Weapons Test Site on August 6, 1985, the fortieth anniversary of the bombing of Hiroshima. Right before a small group of us were arrested for trespassing, Sister Anne McCarthy and I recited the vow of nonviolence together. We felt the desert was an especially appropriate place for monks to pledge nonviolence. I wrote at that time:

Everywhere we could feel our ancestors. All the ancient desert fathers and mothers who had protested the linkage of church and state and said no to militarism were present. All the members of our monastic family who carried the non-military tradition in the early church came to witness. Abba Antony was sitting on a rock. Pachomius peered out of a cave. Syncletica gave her blessing. Martin of Tours smiled.

We proclaimed our vow of nonviolence:

Recognizing the violence in my own heart, yet trusting in the goodness and mercy of God, I vow for one year to practice the nonviolence of Jesus who taught us in the Sermon on the Mount:

"Blessed are the peacemakers, for they shall be called the sons and daughters of God. . . . You have learned how it was said, 'You must love your neighbor and hate your enemy'; but I say to you, love your enemies, and pray for those who persecute you. In this way, you will be daughters and sons of your Creator in heaven."

I vow to carry out in my life the love and example of Jesus:

- by striving for peace within myself and seeking to be a peace-maker in my daily life;
- by refusing to retaliate in the face of provocation and violence;
- by persevering in nonviolence of tongue and heart;
- by living conscientiously and simply so that I do not deprive others of the means to live;
- by actively resisting evil and working nonviolently to abolish war and the causes of war from my own heart and from the face of the earth.

God, I trust in Your sustaining love and believe that just as You gave me the grace and desire to offer this, so You will also bestow abundant grace to fulfill it.

⚬

I Seek the One

Rumi wrote:

> I am neither Christian, Jew, Parsi, nor Muslim. I am neither of the East nor of the West, nor of the land nor of the sea. . . . I have put aside duality, I have seen that the two worlds are one; I seek the One, I know the One, I invoke the One. The One is the First, the One is the Last, the One is Outward, the One is Inward.

Based on that quote, I wish Rumi had been with me last week when I met with a group that wanted to learn about Monasteries of the Heart. We began by reading aloud from the "Introduction" to *The Monastery of the Heart* by Joan Chittister.

We didn't get far into the first paragraph when one woman spoke up: "I always thought that as I aged my faith would get stronger. But now I find myself questioning everything and wondering if there is a God or if this whole existence is just a big joke."

That evoked a lengthy, honest, and privileged discussion on "What is God?"

A whole gamut of beliefs or disbeliefs was present. One woman questioned the whole idea of a personal God and had a hard time grappling with the idea of a God who cared for each individual. Another was adamant in her belief of a personal God because she had experienced such a God in her life. Another spoke and said, "After years of centering prayer, I believe God is in me. . . . I am God." Another admitted that she didn't go through life agonizing on the question of what God is, but went about trying to live a good life and bring mercy, compassion, kindness to everyone she met.

I'm sure Rumi would have been a much more insightful facilitator than myself, but I was so honored to be in the room. This was real God-talk. It wasn't superficial or safe. Here people were wrestling with honest "to the bone" questions. They risked being vulnerable in their search for truth.

I left exhilarated and nourished and more committed to my own questions. Most of all I left feeling part of a genuine monastic movement. Julian of Norwich got it right: "All shall be well, and all shall be well, and all manner of thing shall be well."

❦

Patron of Food

I have a well-earned reputation as a food addict (I prefer connoisseur), one I come by honestly. My mother, thank God, was the goddess of food. I would awaken every morning to biscuits or waffles or pancakes or French toast or sizzling bacon and once over lightly fried eggs or ham sandwiches on fresh rolls. None of this cold cereal stuff. I lived next door to the parochial school I attended so every noon I skipped home to a hot lunch, always fresh, no leftovers. When school ended, I walked into a home filled with the aroma of a just-baked banana cake or jelly cookies or elderberry pie or some special Polish pastry. Every evening we sat down to a homemade meal, no packages ever. And you should hear about Christmas Eve with a feast for 50 family members and Easter and evening snacks and huge family picnics, tables overflowing. Yes, every single event revolved around food, glorious food.

I identify strongly with the exchange in the movie *Last Holiday* where Queen Latifah is discussing food with a gourmet chef. He asks her: "What is the secret of life?" Queen Latifah responds, "I don't know. What is it?" The chef smiles and says simply, "Butter."

In one of his books Ed Hays urges us to consider the Zen monk Pu-Tai, a tenth-century wandering monk, as the patron of feasting. Hays calls Pu-Tai a fat Saint Francis of Assisi. Pu-Tai is the laughing Buddha with the fat belly that greets you in many Chinese restaurants. I was delighted to meet Pu-Tai but still wish we had a patron saint in the Catholic tradition to offset all those gaunt, fasting, ascetic saints. We need someone to remind us that food and feasting is holy.

Finally, here's a story that I consider the purest of wisdom and am committed to emulate on my deathbed:

As a holy monk lay dying, his most trusted disciple asked, "Can I get you anything, Teacher?" The old monk whispered, "Would you go to the market and purchase my favorite pastry." The disciple obliged, and the old monk ate the cake slowly, savoring every morsel. As word spread that the holy one was dying, all the disciples gathered around the bedside and begged, "Give us one final word, Teacher, please." The old monk wiped the crumbs from his lips with the sleeve of his robe and nodded his head. With the disciples hovering in rapt attention, the old monk smacked his lips and said, "My, but this cake is delicious."

CR

The Great Soul

*E*arlier I mentioned how the novel *All Quiet on the Western Front* turned me into a pacifist. Today I'd like to tell you what book turned me into a revolutionary.

But first, I want to tell you about an opera, *Satyagraha* by Philip Glass, that I saw as a film last month. What a gift the Met has given by making its productions available for cinema distribution once the curtain closes on the live performance. I can't fly to New York for every opera, but a movie of the live performance is second best.

The opera itself is a four-hour meditation on Gandhi's early resistance efforts in South Africa. The only lyrics in the opera are from the *Bhagavad Gita*, the sacred text Gandhi memorized and from which he drew his vision for justice without violence. He called his effort *satyagraha*—"truth force." I can't do justice describing the opera, so suffice it to say it was perhaps the most creative production I've ever experienced.

I sat in that dark theater and remembered where I first met Mahatma Gandhi, the Great Soul. I was in my late twenties and picked up *The Essential Gandhi: An Anthology of His Writings on His Life, Work, and Ideas,* edited by Louis Fischer, to take on a bus trip.

If Remarque convinced me that war was wrong, Gandhi showed me how to change sinful and oppressive structures through nonviolent direct action. I remember being so afire with Gandhi's words that I wanted to run up and down the bus shouting his message that only love, courage, and creativity—not violence—can bring about lasting personal and structural transformation. I became a disciple and spent a good part of my life teaching and experimenting with nonviolence and engaging in nonviolent acts of resistance.

What Fisher did with his book, Philip Glass did with the opera. It rekindled the fire. Again I wanted to run into the streets and plead with every Occupy Wall Street demonstrator to see *Satyagraha*. I wanted them to realize that they are part of a long tradition of nonviolent revolution, but, more, I wanted them to experience how essential great art is to social change.

Then I learned that Occupy New York actually staged a rally outside of the Met at the closing performance linking their efforts to Gandhi's historical movement, and that Philip Glass came out and spoke to them. I can't tell you what that bit of news did for my soul. I wish, though, that there had been a special performance for all the demonstrators.

I believe they would have left that opera like I did, uplifted and afire with possibility, more committed to the long haul, affirmed that their nonviolent economic revolution is part of the truth force surging through history. And the opera would have shown them how to hold on with beauty.

As Ruth Rimm reminds us, "The role of the artist is to visualize the dreams of humanity, not just its nightmares. The role of art is to transform despair into delight and helplessness into hope. In troubled times, the artist serves as a voice that cries in the wilderness, not a voice that terrorizes in the wilderness."

CR

On Kindness

The Talmud teaches,
"The beginning and end of Torah
is performing acts
of loving kindness."

And the Dalai Lama preaches,
"My only religion
is kindness."

And a Christian mystic wrote
"Do you want to be a saint?
Be kind, be kind, be kind."

I don't know about you
but I find it easier to memorize
the catechism and cite quotes
in the *Summa* to prove the existence of God
and wax eloquent with insights
into the scriptures
and meditate for hours
and keep a chart of how many times
others have broken the Ten Commandments
and attend church regularly, front pew.

That's how I measure religion and sanctity.

How about you?
Being kind is too simplistic
when it comes to heavy matters
like religion and sainthood.
To tell you the truth
I've tried it off and on
but being kind to people
who don't deserve it
only fills me with anger and bitterness.

Besides, if being kind were the measure,
anyone could be a saint
and we know that's impossible.
Don't we?

CR

An Image for the Heart

A quote that has haunted me over the years is from Albert Camus, who wrote, "A person's life purpose is nothing more than to rediscover, through the detours of art, or love, or passionate work, those one or two images in the presence of which the heart first opened."

Since I read that quote a few years ago, I have struggled to find an image or memory where my heart first broke open and altered my life. It was kind of embarrassing not to have the image appear immediately. After all, I came to the monastery to discover myself. Are all those years of sitting for nothing? All those prayers and chants only emptiness?

Then an image suddenly appeared. I was probably five or six years old and in my third year of kindergarten. We lived next door to the school and convent and were very close to the nuns, so I began school at three. My mother always said, "You were bored, and we didn't know what to do with you," but when I look back it was probably because my mother was so sick with asthma, had me and my eighteen-month-old brother and a third baby on the way, and the sisters were trying to help. Anyway, by my third year I was a pro at reading and recesses and whatever else they teach you in kindergarten. Suffice it to say that by seniority alone I ruled the roost.

The image that appeared was of me laughing at Marian. Little Marian lived across the street from me, was a bit slow in learning, and kind of chubby. She was the type of child that is often the butt of other children's meanness—a rather defenseless sort that is an easy scapegoat. That day poor Marian had wet her pants.

I can still see the other children pointing their fingers at her and laughing. I also knew a moment of decision—what I did could alter the situation. Well, what I did was join in the laughing. My friend Marian, the girl I played with after school, sat there with tears streaming down her face while I laughed. I knew immediately that I had committed a grave sin: I lacked courage in a crowd, I chose to betray a friend, I caused deep suffering to an innocent.

And there it was—the image that first broke open my heart. When I examine the direction of my life, it is no stretch to say that since that incident I began a lifelong pilgrimage of atonement. The purpose of my life was clear: be a voice for the innocent, resist the crowd's approval and allure, hold fast to friendship and loyalty.

CR

One Good Deed

"I don't think I believe in God," the young man said. He was my nephew, and we were having a drink together after a round of golf.

My mind panics during conversations like this; it searches frantically through all its file drawers to come up with something life giving. Thank God I remembered a story from Dostoyevsky's *The Brothers Karamazov*. In this scene the saintly Father Zosima is counseling a woman who has lost her faith. The monk listens attentively and then tells her to forget about believing in God. Instead, the wise Zosima sends her home and tells her that each day she should do a loving deed for another person.

So, I told him the story. I prefer it to a lot of theological posturing on faith. The story is just another way of saying that God is love and when we love we imitate God whether we rationally believe or not. It's another take on the reality that God is within everyone and everything and what we do to creation we do to God whether we name it that or not. It's another way of reminding us that faith doesn't exist in the abstract, but only in deeds of kindness and love. And it's absolutely the best spiritual practice possible. Try to imagine if seekers everywhere practiced this spiritual discipline—do one loving deed each day.

Dostoyevsky could imagine it. He wrote, "Love God's young creation, love it as a whole, and every grain of sand in it. Love every leaf, every ray of God. Love animals, love every plant and everything. If you love everything, the mystery of God will be revealed to you in things. . . . And finally, you will love the whole universe with a comprehensive, all-embracing love."

I don't believe in much, but I have abiding faith that by practicing love the mystery of God will be revealed to me.

As for my nephew, all I can say is that he listened and followed the story with a rhetorical "But what is love?" His question made me smile. You only have to observe him for a few minutes with his four children—loving deed after loving deed—to know his question was for the sake of argument only. There is no doubt in my mind that he believes in the one thing necessary. I've seen it in action.

○᠀

Songbird Smugglers

During Holy Week, the last week of Lent, we spend sacred time with Jesus the prisoner—condemned, stripped, beaten by the guards, tortured, and killed.

I have minor jail experiences for civil disobedience. My strongest impressions are of boredom, just sitting and waiting with nothing to do for a week in a Harrisburg, Pennsylvania, facility; fear, from an overnight stay in the Washington, DC, jail when we had to walk through the male section and were greeted with a scenario out of Dante's underworld. And I vividly remember one long ride after another DC arrest in a stifling hot, airless paddy wagon that reeked of vomit.

Based on these brief brushes with prison, I expect those serving long sentences to emerge less human than when they walked into the cell. The system is designed to dehumanize.

That's why I never tire of telling the story of the special prison in Uruguay where political prisoners were not permitted to whistle, smile, sing, greet other inmates, or draw pictures of pregnant women, butterflies, stars, or birds. One day a schoolteacher who had been tortured and jailed "for having ideological ideas" is visited by his five-year-old daughter. She brings him a drawing of birds, but the guards destroy it at the gate. The following week she brings him a drawing of trees, which are not forbidden, and it gets through. Her father praises the drawing and asks, "But what are those colored circles in the trees, half-hidden by branches. Are they oranges?" The little girl puts her finger to her mouth, "Shhh." And she whispers in her father's ear, "Don't you see that they are eyes? They're the eyes of the birds that I've smuggled in for you."

As I am writing this, I get an email that I open. It's from Muin, a prison chaplain who receives free issues of *The Monastic Way* and other materials from The Joan Chittister Fund for Prisoners. She writes, "You have no idea the help this has brought us here at the county jails. . . . Some women in prison have actually written to me many times on the lessons they have learned from *The Monastic Way*. The biggest surprise, however, are the male inmates. *The Monastic Way*, as one of them put it, "has softened my heart."

And there it is: Why are we so intent on supporting those in prisons? Because smuggled songbirds can "soften the heart." And a soft and tender heart is all it takes to become new. It is why we pray during Lent, "Give us a new heart, O God, and put a new spirit with us. Remove our hearts of stone and give us hearts of flesh."

☙

Nonviolent Hissing

The support demonstrated by so many for sisters in the United States following the Vatican announcement that it was "reforming" the Leadership Conference of Women Religious is both challenging and humbling.

Let us memorize this story from Anthony De Mello, and may it kindle in us holy creativity:

A snake in the village had bitten so many people that few dared go into the fields. Such was the Teacher's holiness that she was said to have tamed the snake and persuaded it to practice the discipline of nonviolence.

It did not take long for the villagers to discover the snake had become harmless. They took to hurling stones at it and dragging it about by its tail.

The badly battered snake crawled into the Teacher's house one night to complain. The Teacher said, "Friend, you've stopped frightening people—that's bad!"

"But it was you who taught me to practice the discipline of nonviolence!"

"I told you to stop hurting—not to stop hissing!"

Point: Authentic nonviolence does not harm, but it does know when to hiss. It hisses loud and long at every system and structure that trods the weak and powerless underfoot. It hisses so strongly and with such persistence that governments topple and dictatorships dissolve.

When the Filipino people—armed with rosary beads—toppled the Marcos government by kneeling in front of tanks, that was a hiss.

When tens of thousands of students poured into Tiananmen Square bearing this placard: "Although you trod a thousand underfoot, I shall be the one thousand and first"—that was a hiss.

When Theresa Kane stood before Pope John Paul II at the National Shrine in Washington, DC, in 1979, and called for inclusion of women in all the ministries of the church, that was a hiss.

Nonviolence, then, can never be equated with passivity; it is the essence of courage, creativity, and action. Nonviolence does, however, require patience and a passionate commitment to seek justice and truth no matter the cost.

Let us pray, then: God give us an urgent patience, God give us a "wild patience," God give us a "revolutionary patience." And most of all, God, enlighten us with imaginative ways to hiss.

ભ્

Question after Question

As May, the month dedicated to Mary, winds down, I'd like to share this thought: Have you ever thought about Mary's first response to the angel? It's a question. "How can this be?" Think about it, a young, uneducated, teenage girl questioning God. Not even a rabbi or Pharisee or even a high priest, but God. In Mary's litany we call her many things: mystical rose, star of hope, refuge of sinners. How about adding, "bearer of courageous questions"?

Then let's imitate her by asking at least one of the following questions until we get an answer that satisfies. How can this be: that we as church still legitimize war? Is not the core message of Jesus nonviolence? How can this be: that women are not allowed to be ordained? Are they not baptized? How can this be: that Christians go to church Sunday after Sunday, yet hunger and poverty increase in the land? How can this be: that church documents teach that gays and lesbians are "intrinsically disordered"? Are not all human beings made in the image of God? How can this be: that some questions are forbidden in the church? Didn't Jesus himself ask question after question and provoke questions in others?

As Thomas Merton notes:

Questions cannot go unanswered unless they first be asked. And there is a far worse anxiety, a far worse insecurity, which comes from being afraid to ask the right questions—because they might turn out to have no answers. One of the moral diseases we communicate to one another in society comes from huddling together in the pale light of an insufficient answer to a question we are afraid to ask.

We must not be afraid to ask the difficult questions.

℞

Theopoetry

It's called theopoetry. That's what I've been doing for years and didn't realize it until I read *Dorothee Sölle Essential Writings*, selected with an introduction by Dianne L. Oliver. The late German liberation theologian and mystic Sölle had a significant impact on my spiritual development, and reading the book was like visiting a dear old friend.

Sölle explains that, for her, theology "is much more art than science." More oriented to poetry—"to the fresh, to the surprise, to the aha—rather than to the abstract, rational, and neutral." Sölle urges us to communicate with God in images, in stories, and in narratives that spring from the real, from our everyday experiences. She cites the Jewish tradition as doing this kind of theology—always telling a story rather than arguing a theological thesis to explain the unexplainable. She cites Eastern religions—think Rumi, Hafiz, Rabia—as developing theology through theopoetry.

In the poem that follows, Sölle takes an actual event, something she really experienced, and through a poem articulates an expanding theology of prayer. She explains, "I want to learn to take what is here now, to see and hear it, which is to say, to live more attentively. . . . To be attentive also in everyday occurrences and to listen, to inquire, and to interpret attentively in a conversation—that is what makes for a poem."

And I saw a man on 126th Street
broom in hand
sweeping eight feet of the street
Meticulously he removed garbage and dirt
from a tiny area
in the midst of a huge expanse
of garbage and dirt.
And I saw a man on 126th Street
sorrow sat on his back
sweeping eight feet of the street
Wear and tear showed on his arms
in a city
where only crazy folk
find something to hope in.
And I saw a man on 126th Street
broom in hand
There are many ways to offer prayer.
With a broom in the hand
is one I had hitherto
not seen before.

I think my book *Between Two Souls: Conversations with Ryōkan* is a way of doing theopoetry. I read a poem by the great nineteenth-century Japanese Zen monk Ryōkan and then responded from my own lived experiences. Here's an example:

Ryōkan wrote:

If someone asks
My abode
I reply:

"The east edge of
The Milky Way."

Like a drifting cloud,
Bound by nothing:
I just let go
Giving myself up
To the whim of the wind.

I wrote:

If someone asks
Me where I live
I answer
"Does a monk
own a key?

If I hear
A child cry
There is
My home."

❦

Going Home

I'm on retreat this week and came upon this poem by the Japanese
Buddhist monk Shinsho:

Does one really have to fret
About enlightenment?
No matter what road I travel,
I'm going home.

When I think of all the retreats and lectures I have attended, all the books I've read about attaining enlightenment, and then I read this. When I remember the angst over finding a spiritual path that fits, and then I read this. Are all those years of experimenting with spiritual stuff necessary in order to come to the simplicity of this poem? Or do we make the journey home to self a difficult maze when it's actually a familiar neighborhood street?

Speaking of neighborhood streets, I live in a neighborhood that most people are afraid to drive through, though my particular block is undergoing a transformation. On the next block, probably one of the top five worst blocks in the city, lived a ninety-year-old woman—all by herself—who did what she could to make it a human neighborhood. For years she decorated the front of her house in honor of every holiday, holy day, and season change. I mean *really* decorated—plastic flowers and lights and flags and banners and bunny rabbits and huge lit hearts for Valentine's Day. If anyone kept the liturgical church year it was she.

Here's the thing: no one ever stole a decoration, vandalized the property, or bothered an old white woman who lived alone and called a lot of attention to herself. She was fearless. When gangs of teens parked on her porch, she didn't call the police. She went out with a broom and kicked them off the front step. When someone threw wet laundry on bushes to dry, she rang their doorbell holding a rope clothesline and asked, "Can I show you how to hang clothes outside?" When drug deals were taking place in the street, she'd open the front door and ream them out in language salty enough to make the dealers blush. Every single morning she was out at crack of dawn sweeping her porch and sidewalk, bringing an inch of order to the chaos. She was kind to the neighborhood children, and they respected her tender toughness. She died last month. She was a personal hero of mine, a dame who lived Daniel Berrigan's teaching, "Decide where you stand, and stand there."

CR

Becoming a Book

On June 5, 2012, the day after Ray Bradbury died, we were sitting around the lunch table discussing his impact on our lives. Our talk centered on his most famous book, *Fahrenheit 451*, the novel in which Bradbury predicts the time when television and electronic devices and sound bites become the diet of the population turning humans into mindless, easily manipulated beings. In this society firemen burn all books and all houses that contain books. Toward the end of the novel we meet a group of people who resist this destruction of history and beauty and civilization itself by memorizing an entire book, by becoming the book itself.

Naturally, one of the sisters at the table asked, "If you found yourself in the *Fahrenheit 451* world, what book would you become?

Sue jumped right in, "I might choose *Thirst* by Mary Oliver. I love the poems and prose in that book."

I said, "Off the top of my head, I might choose *Journals of a Solitude* by May Sarton, but I'd like to think about it a while." People nodded their heads, yes, they'd like to think about it a while.

So, I have been thinking about it. The next book that came to mind was *All Quiet on the Western Front* by Erich Maria Remarque. As I said before, that World War I novel turned me into a pacifist, and I would want to offer the same opportunity to every human being.

Next I thought about *The Catcher in the Rye*. At a certain age every person would benefit by meeting the pure-of-heart Holden Caulfield. Then I thought about *Siddhartha* by Hermann Hesse and remembered the Buddha's impact on my life's journey. How about the poems of Ryōkan? *A Theology of Liberation* by Gustavo Gutiérrez? *The Essential Gandhi*? Gosh, I'd have to become a library.

I always intended to page through the list of books I've read, and when I opened that notebook there was an introductory page titled

"Books That Have Influenced Me." I'd forgotten about it, but years ago I listed fifteen books that shaped me. Sure enough, all those I've mentioned so far were listed, but the one that popped into my heart wasn't a book at all, it was a short story, *Where Love Is, There God Is Also* by Leo Tolstoy. Whew, I wasn't sure I could memorize a book, but a short story is possible.

I remember when I first read the story. I was in eighth grade, and we had these *Prose and Poetry* books that we used for English class, reading most of the contents aloud. In this story Tolstoy's protagonist is a poor cobbler who has lost his entire family. He is despondent and without hope. Someone suggests that he read the New Testament, and when he does, he is taken with the words of Jesus. One night, while asleep, he hears the voice of Jesus saying, "I am going to visit you tomorrow." Martin wakes up a new man and sits by the window awaiting the visit. He only meets three people that day: an old soldier shovels his sidewalk, and Martin invites him in for tea and conversation; a destitute mother and child are freezing because they have no coat or shawl, and Martin finds a coat for the boy and gives the mother a coin so she can repossess her shawl from the pawn shop; a young boy is caught trying to steal an apple from a peddler, and Martin patches up the conflict and offers to pay for the boy's apple. When evening comes, Martin is disappointed that Jesus did not appear but opens the scripture again. Suddenly he hears, "Martin, Martin, did you not recognize me?" And the old soldier, the mother and child, and the young boy and peddler appear briefly in the room. When he looks down at the scripture it is open to Matthew 25:35, "I was hungry and you fed me, naked and you clothed me, a stranger and you took me in. What you have done to the least of my sisters and brothers, you have done to me."

Until that short story, God, for me, was locked up in the blue sky called heaven or in a gold box in the church called a tabernacle. God is in people? Especially in poor people? That story was a revolution. It planted a seed in me and set my life's compass.

CR

A Healthy Path

How do you know if you're on a healthy spiritual path? I always use as my measure the words of an unidentified mystic, mentioned above, "Do you want to be a saint? Be kind, be kind, be kind." It's a good indicator of whether I'm on a healthy path or, despite the shelves of spiritual books, lost in a pathless jungle.

The other day I read "Ten Signs of Progress on the Spiritual Path," an article by Elizabeth Lesser, cofounder of Omega Institute for Holistic Studies. Her first sign of spiritual growth is Obuntubotho. She writes:

> When Bishop Desmond Tutu introduced Nelson Mandela at his inauguration as the new president of South Africa, he described him as being a man who had *Obuntubotho*. "Obuntubotho," he said, "is the essence of being human. You know when it is there and when it is absent. It speaks about humanness, gentleness, putting yourself out on behalf of others, being vulnerable. It embraces compassion and toughness. It recognizes that my humanity is bound up in ours, for we can only be human together." Obuntubotho is the first sign of progress on the spiritual path.

Lesser's other signs of a healthy spirituality are living in truth, being real and honest, accepting pain as part of life, serving others, becoming more conscious of the interconnectedness of all things, accepting the paradox that we are both loved and alone, celebrating the ordinary, and putting on the mantle of God's optimism.

I agreed with all of her signs, although I might put Obuntubotho as number ten—the culmination of spiritual growth. Would I add any others? Well, I cry a lot, so I'm hoping that the gift of tears is a sign. As Joan Chittister writes, "Tears attune us to ourselves and tears attune us to the rest of the human race as well. Once we ourselves have suffered, the suffering of others falls upon our softened hearts and we become more human members of the human race."

I'd also add lightness of being—am I able to laugh at myself and the endless games I play, like "how to measure progress on the spiritual path"? There's nothing worse than a seeker who takes herself too seriously.

ༀ

A Healthy Path

The monk-poet Ryōkan writes:

> You mustn't suppose
> I never mingle in the world
> of humankind—
> It's simply that I prefer
> To enjoy myself alone.

Me too, Ryōkan. I have to say the best hours of my day are when I can sit in my study in early morning and just read and write and think. I enjoy playing golf alone and going to movies by myself. I'm still not totally crazy about eating alone or taking vacations by myself. At work I spend long hours alone planning, writing, and editing—there are days when fewer than thirty minutes are spent in conversations with co-workers.

I'd like to think that I'm developing a "hermit heart," where I'm more at home with me, happier in my own company. And that's a good thing, as long as I'm not using silence and solitude as an escape from the world of humankind.

The hermit that I'm most attracted to is the one described by Catherine de Hueck Doherty in her book *Poustinia*. She writes about the Russian hermit, a *poustinik*, who lives alone with God but is not a solitary. Rather, this Eastern Christian hermit is attached to a local community and serves humanity through a life of prayer, fasting, and availability. It's availability that makes this type of hermit different. The *poustinik* is available whenever there are communal needs, such as a village fire or harvest time. And, most important, the *poustinik* is always available to those who knock on the hermitage door. Always the *poustinik* is present to share a kind word, some food and drink, good conversation and encouragement. Always the *poustinik* listens to what the visitor really needs and attempts to assist.

So, I may prefer my own company, but if I have a true hermit heart, the needs of others take precedence. The silence and solitude are a sham if I get irritable or testy, for instance, when I'm reading and the phone rings or I'm engrossed in a project and someone interrupts me.

From what I've read about him, Ryōkan was a beautiful wandering *poustinik*. He lived alone, meditating and writing poems, but the door was always open to the visitor in need and to the children who just wanted to play.

I may never become a *poustinik*, but I do hope this movement to preferring my own company is a first step toward a hermit heart and not a step backward into the more selfish.

Oh, there's a knock on my study door. See what I mean? This is what I prefer, being alone with my keyboard and with me, but then there is a second knock. . . .

◌

Who's Rising?

*L*ast month I watched the taped PBS show of comedian Ellen DeGeneres receiving the 2012 Mark Twain Award. Ellen, of course, is a great advocate of dancing. A dance by Ellen and often a guest is the signature of her afternoon talk show, *The Ellen DeGeneres Show*.

So almost every person honoring Ellen did a dance. Some did it gracefully; others did it self-consciously, kind of mocking their own movements. Often you heard nervous laughter in the audience when those on the stage began to shake their hips. Dancing, it seemed, made some dancers and some in the audience uncomfortable, embarrassed even. So, what is it that prevents so many of us from enjoying one of life's greatest pleasures?

We all know the answer, don't we? We're not comfortable in our bodies. We got bad messages about our gracefulness or lack thereof when growing up. We worry about what others will think about our two left feet and complete lack of rhythm. We don't want to look ridiculous. We imagine that everyone in the room is staring at us and is either laughing at us or embarrassed for us. We lack freedom.

"The dancer's body is simply the luminous manifestation of the soul," said Irene Duncan. Ouch! Now, there's a thought for all of us non-dancers to ponder. Which brings me to the point. Eve Ensler, the author of *The Vagina Monologues,* invited every woman on earth to one gigantic dance party on February 14, 2013. She called it One Billion Rising and expects that many to attend. Her points are simple: one in three women on this planet will be raped or beaten in her lifetime. One billion women violated is an atrocity. One billion women rising is a revolution.

I love acts of protest that both resist evil and encourage creativity. I've attended too many demonstrations that were nothing but endurance contests—hours of one long boring speech after another. "I pray these people never win the revolution," I'd say to myself. "I do not want them in charge of the earth. There will be no joy, no play, no creativity, no imagination."

Now along comes Eve Ensler asking "one billion women and those who love them to walk out, dance, rise up, and demand an end to violence against women."

My plea is that all of us get over our self-absorption and do something revolutionary for our daughters yet to come—gather in a city park, put on the music, turn up the volume, and dance. Just dance.

∞

Christ Comes Uninvited

A friend was cleaning out and found a homily that I gave for one of our sisters a number of years ago. She gave it to me, and I was reminded how important friends and mentors are in life. This sister, Ethelreda was her name, was my first principal when, at the age of nineteen, I was sent to teach fourth grade in one of our schools.

In that classroom was a little boy who was very poor and a troublemaker, probably had ADHD, though we didn't diagnose it then. His mother was mentally ill. There was no father. Leif demanded a lot of attention in the classroom and there is no disputing that I favored him and gave him lots of my time. He created a lot of havoc and some of the parents and most of the faculty wanted him expelled.

In those days we had thirty minutes of recreation each evening when we could talk and take walks in the playground if the weather was good. Many evenings Sister Ethelreda would ask me to walk with her. And she did it for a specific reason. "You must take care of Leif," she would repeat over and over. "Don't pay attention to what anyone says about him. We are here to help people like Leif and his mother. We must help them. Sisters are here for the poor." Over and over. Step after step. Walk after walk.

Leif got through fourth grade thanks to Sister Ethelreda. But I know it cost her—it was a very strong faculty. For me, however, it was a lifelong lesson in what later was called the preferential option for the poor.

Which bring us to Christmas and God's reminder that we are here for the poor. Thomas Merton said it best in *Raids on the Unspeakable*:

Into this world, this demented inn, in which there is no room for him at all, Christ comes uninvited. . . . His place is with those who do not belong, who are rejected by power because they are regarded as weak, those who are discredited, who are denied the status of persons, tortured and exterminated. With those for whom there is no room, Christ is personally present in this world. He is mysteriously present in those for whom there seems to be nothing but the world at its worst.

I know all of you have a special room in your hearts for "those for whom there seems to be nothing but the world at its worst." Let's all do something to make this Christmas less harsh, a little softer.

℃

A Few Postcards: Lenten Reflection

Why did we choose the name Monasteries of the Heart for this movement?

We did so because monasticism is a heart-centered spirituality. Monks are not so much intent on knowledge about things outside themselves (good as that is) but about inner knowledge, about knowing their hearts.

In the desert tradition there's a story about two monks: Abba Poemen said to Abba Joseph, "Tell me how to become a monk." He said, "If you want to find rest here below, and hereafter, in all circumstances say, 'Who am I?' and do not judge anyone."

My nephew gave me a book for Christmas called *PostSecret*. He thought it might offer some writing prompts. The book is a compilation of secrets revealed anonymously on postcards to Frank Warren. He started the project in 2004, asking people to send him a postcard with a secret written on it—"a regret, fear, betrayal, desire, confession or childhood humiliation . . . as long as it is true, and you have never shared it with anyone." We all have secrets, and we all know the courage it takes to reveal them. Secrets, we know, are cannibals that eat you alive from the inside. Often, just the sharing results in some healing.

In a sense that's how monastic spirituality is supposed to work. It's like writing ourselves one postcard after another, a lifetime of revealing our deepest secrets to ourselves. Secrets like: What really motivates my actions? Do my words and deeds truly reveal what's in my heart? Am I the person I pretend to be in public? What am I ashamed of? What don't I like about myself and why? What do I really believe, and can I say it aloud? How do I treat others and why do I treat them that way?

Yes, it's a lifetime of not flinching from the question, Who am I? The saving grace is that all this inner work is done while being held in the tender arms of God. That's why the practice of *lectio divina* (sacred reading for self-knowledge) is at the heart of monastic spirituality.

A few beautiful things could happen if you are intent on forming a monastic heart. One, the more you know about yourself, the less you will judge others, as Abba Joseph so wisely attests. Two, you can come to great freedom of spirit—all the chains that held you captive are unlocked. You are yourself and "it is good." And third, you could become the monastic heart described by Joan Chittister as "a place without boundaries, a place where the truth of the oneness of the human community shatters all barriers, opens all doors, refuses all prejudices, welcomes all strangers, and listens to all voices."

Which brings us to Lent. Although the Rule of Saint Benedict says that the life of a monastic "ought always to be a Lent," these forty days are a sacred time to do a monastic heart checkup.

The promise is spoken aloud to us on Ash Wednesday: "And I will give you a new heart, and I will put a new spirit in you. I will take out your stony, stubborn heart and give you a tender, responsive heart" (Ezek 36:26). All we have to do is write a few postcards.

CR

Dance for Women

Valentine's Day 2013 was a love note from women across the globe to each other.

I'm still smiling about thirty of us dancing around the block where we work to the tune of "When the Saints Go Marching In." Only we changed it to "Oh, when the women begin to rise, oh, when the women begin to rise, I want to be in that number, when the women begin to rise." We banged drums and shook rattles and banged on pots and pans and danced.

We joined a line dance that stretched across 250 countries with thousands of events involving some twenty-five million participants. All of us were part of One Billion Rising, an international call led by Eve Ensler's V-Day organization to end violence against women and girls.

Women danced in all seven thousand islands of the Philippines, in fifty cities of Turkey, in one hundred risings in Italy, in the Democratic Republic of the Congo, in Ethiopia, in South Africa, in Albania, in the Warsaw Railway Center, in Hong Kong, across India, in Afghanistan, in Israel, in 135 risings in the United Kingdom, and in city after city in the United States. Some even risked their lives to dance in places where it's forbidden.

Eve Ensler, founder of One Billion Rising, explains:

The diversity of the risings is beyond anything we could have imagined: the carnival queen in Rio de Janeiro, the queen mother of Bhutan, prime ministers of Australia and Croatia, members of the European parliament, lamas, nuns, union leaders, avatars in Second Life, Zumba dancers, classical dancers in Karachi, cast members of *Wicked* and *The Lion King* on Broadway, women in the Andes, 200 women in a parking lots in Kamloops, British Columbia, Iranian teenagers

in their bedrooms, thousands of Afghani women dressed in
OBR scarves, Filipino domestic workers in Saudi Arabia,
people on bridges, in buses, prisons, squares, in stadiums, in
churches, theaters.

It was a massive and most creative celebration of sisterhood. I
know I will never be the same.

I am more outraged than ever that one in three women in the
world will be raped or abused at some point in life. I am more
hopeful than ever that woman will demand an end to this violence.
I am more committed than ever to a world where all women are
safe and free and treated with justice and dignity. And most of all,
because of the dance I feel more connected than ever to women
everywhere.

Eve Ensler said it all, "Dance with your body, for your body, for
the bodies of women and the earth." And women did.

⚬⚬

For Beginners Only: Feast of Benedict

The feast of Saint Benedict, the founder of Western monastic life,
is March 21. The Rule of Saint Benedict is a spiritual classic
that has been used by millions of seekers for over fifteen hundred
years. A line in the rule that I like to visit frequently is found in
the last chapter, where he instructs us to "keep this little rule that
we have written for beginners. After that you can set out for the
loftier summits."

When I was younger, I looked at that line and said to myself, "He
wrote this way of life for beginners in the spiritual life. I've been
at this life for years. Why am I still following it? Am I spiritually
challenged or what?"

But now I think Benedict was writing that tongue in cheek,
cleverly reminding us that a "beginner's heart" is the one thing

necessary for this way of life. And we only kid ourselves when we imagine ascending loftier summits.

Many spiritual giants would agree. From the desert fathers and mothers we have this saying: "Abba Poemen said of Abba Pior that every day he made a fresh beginning."

And Thomas Merton writes about the monastic life, "There are only three stages to this work: to be a beginner, to be more of a beginner, and to be only a beginner."

So that's what this feast day is all about. We get a chance to thank Saint Benedict for introducing a way of life that celebrates falling down and getting up, falling down and getting up. We raise a toast to never getting it quite right. We join the choir of monastic women and men, both living and from ages past, in singing, "Happy feast day to all of us beginners." Happy feast, everyone.

ଔ

What Do You Seek?

As you know, Saint Benedict listed only one criterion for accepting members into the community: "Do you seek God?" That was all he cared about.

But what does it mean to seek God? Does the search ever have an end? How do we know when we've found God, as if God could be absent? Then a friend, Therese, told me a story.

Therese's father had Alzheimer's. Although he couldn't remember much, he always remembered her phone number. So, one day she got a call from him, and he was very distressed because he had lost something. Therese told him that she would go to the nursing home where he lived as soon as she finished work. When she arrived, he was going from corner to corner in his small room, looking inside the pillows of the sofa, opening dresser drawers. Therese began looking too. Finally, she asked, "Dad, what is it that you are looking for?'" And her father replied, "I don't know, but when we find it we'll both know."

I figure that's about as good an answer I can give to the question "What do you seek?"—I don't know, but when I find it, I'll know.

CR

Koan of the Day

I found this lovely quote by Terry Tempest Williams from her *Ode to Slowness* in which she dreams of making a living by watching light like Monet and Vermeer and being "a caretaker of silence, a connoisseur of stillness, a listener of wind where each dialect is not only heard but understood."

Isn't that a beautiful profession—watching light and being a caretaker of silence. Someone should be paid to do it. Hmmm . . . maybe that's what monks are for.

As you know by now, I'm always trying to figure out who or what monks are. So I was grateful to come across this definition by Cistercian monk Dom André Louf:

> What is a monk?
> A monk is someone who every day asks:
> "What is a monk?"

Now there's a koan for you. God willing, I still have a few years left to figure it out. Of course, if I figure it out, I may no longer be a monk.

CR

On Reading an Obit

Tragic is too facile a word to use when your fifteen-year-old boy dies. It's best to be silent, you think. Don't try to explain the impossible, just be silent and absorb the pain. And yet you want others to understand the terrible grief and loss you feel. So, you write a beautiful obituary for the newspaper and tell the world how much you loved your dear son, how proud you were of him, and what an impact his brief life made on so many. You talk about your son's unusual gifts. You tell them about his talent for music and all the awards he won for piano. You tell about his leadership skills and how he loved to travel, recently returning from China. You say he loved big ideas, and you include a picture of a smiling, handsome young man.

And then, in the obit, you add this paragraph. "Jesse was a member of his local Presbyterian Church, where he participated in Sunday School and the youth mission trip. As a young gay man, Jesse found great support at his church and among his friends and family, and he looked forward hopefully to the day when there would be full equality for all."

I had never seen courageous words like these in a local obituary. I didn't know your son, but I sat and wept. I wept for you and your great goodness. I am so sorry for your unbearable loss and emptiness. I wept for Jesse and his courage to embrace who he was. I wept for all gay and lesbian and transgender people who never experienced this parental acceptance. I wept for all the hard-hearted or misguided people who spew hatred and cause suffering for the Jesses of this world. I wept a prayer of gratitude for churches like his that welcomed Jesse for who he was, a child of God like any other. And I wept for the sins of churches like my own who through their exclusion and cruel pronouncements help make life a hell for beautiful young people like Jesse.

Though I wept, I found your words to be healing and godlike. Thank you.

❧

About a Table

I'm reading Pat Schneider's *Where the Light Gets In: Writing as Spiritual Practice*. Today she talks about using the poem "Perhaps the World Ends Here" by Joy Harjo in her writing workshops.

She asks her students to concentrate on the first line of the poem, "The world begins at a kitchen table," and to write about a table.

Here's my try:

> I've never sat at my table. I'm not even sure it exists, but I keep searching for it—the perfect writer's table. I think I want something made of fine dark brown wood about five or six feet long and two to three feet wide. I don't want any drawers beneath it, maybe a small one under the top to hold my pens. And the legs can't be too bulky or too thin or too ornate—but I want a sturdy, simple, rustic look. I want lots of space for papers and books and my Mac laptop. I don't want my legs banging into anything. Maybe I'll put my ceramic muse in the left-hand corner. Every furniture store I visit, I look for the perfect desk. I often Google "writer's desks." Just like I Google "gifts for writers" and am a sucker for ads pushing "poet's blouse" or "poet's capris." I'm positive that if I find the desk I seek, I will finally finish the three books that I started years ago. Depending, of course, on whether I also find the perfect pen.

❧

The Waiting Room

I spent four hours in a mental health and detox unit recently, waiting to see if someone I care about very deeply could commit himself. He knew he needed help, but that doesn't always guarantee that residential help will be given. Two young adults, for example, were refused admission to the detox unit because they had just been there in April. Instead, they were given sheets of paper with phone numbers for a dozen or so agencies in the state and told to call. I sat by the young woman, a heroin addict, who sobbed through every phone call as she was told, "Sorry, we cannot take you."

We watched person after person enter the waiting room, most of them coming all by themselves—no families, no loved ones, no resources. *Nada.*

As far as I could tell, the young man and woman went back to the drug house where they had been staying. There was no help available. The person I came with was admitted. When I left around midnight, the room was still filled with the desperately poor, addicted, and ill—all waiting.

I've thought about the people in that waiting room all week long. I marvel at their will to stay alive in this vale of tears. What keeps you going when no one else cares whether you live or die?

I rage at the budget cuts for the most vulnerable in our society. The money wasted on meaningless wars while a pittance is allotted to the mentally ill, the homeless, the addicted. And what can be done about this hardness of heart that grips the nation? The absence of compassion for the suffering among us?

I'm writing this in the morning right before prayer. In a few minutes I will intone "This is the day our God has made." The sisters I pray with will answer, "Let us rejoice and be glad." Sometimes the words catch in my throat.

☙

The Impossible Dream

Want to know a secret about burnout? It's in this story:

A seeker searched for years to know the secret of achievement and success in human life. One night in a dream a Sage appeared bearing the answer to the secret.

The Sage said simply, "Stretch out your hand and reach what you can."

But the seeker replied, "No, it can't be that. It must be something harder, something more satisfying to the human spirit."

The Sage replied softly, "You are right, it is something harder. It is this: stretch out your hand and reach what you cannot."

I've been involved in a lot of peace and justice initiatives in my life and have seen people burn out because they didn't believe or understand this story. The story says it simply and clearly: There are things that are unreachable. For example, you can't save another person. You can't bring the world to peace. You can't end poverty. You can't stop war. If you believe you can "save" a person or situation, burnout lies in wait somewhere down the road.

The story sets us on a more difficult path. It asks us to strive for the unreachable—year after year after year—without attachment to results or success. A meaningful life is all about faithful effort to reach for the unreachable. Rubem Alves said it well, "We must live by the love of what we will never see."

Part Two

THIS I BELIEVE

Journal Entries, 2013–2019

ભ

Nirvana Here and Now

What is the Dalai Lama's favorite prayer? When asked that question the Dalai Lama said it is the one recited by the bodhisattvas, the enlightened ones. A bodhisattva is able to reach nirvana but delays it out of compassion for those suffering on earth. The prayer is from the eighth-century Buddhist monk-poet Shantideva:

> For as long as space endures,
> And for as long as living beings remain,
> Until then may I, too, abide
> To dispel the misery of the world.

Old Monk would like to delay the final departure into eternal bliss, too. Often, she wishes that she were younger, because there is so much to do yet, so many wounds that need balm. Then there are lesser motives like loving this earth too much, if that's even possible.

Old Monk loves it all: sizzling potato pancakes, a sunset on Lake Erie, a new author to explore, laughter with friends, hitting a great golf shot. Almost all those who Old Monk talks to say they would not choose to live forever. As for Old Monk, she'd choose to stay. She agrees with Gibran: "Yes, there is Nirvana; it is in leading your sheep to a green pasture, and in putting your child to sleep, and in writing the last line of your poem." And Old Monk would add: "in being one with all those in misery and pain, too." This is enough.

∾

Awestruck

A couple months ago a friend sent Old Monk the video *Dylan Winter and the Starling Murmurations,* which captured the evening dance of starlings. Old Monk was awestruck. How is it possible that every evening 300,000 starlings gather at the same spot in the sky, dance this incredible ballet, and then nosedive to roost for the night.

Or how about this fact: If a star is a million light years away (our Milky Way galaxy is about one hundred thousand light years wide), we are observing the way it looked a million years ago, not the way it looks today. And that's a close star.

In his Rule, Saint Benedict enumerated twelve steps of humility. He wrote that the first degree of humility is the awe of God. Old Monk doesn't know why it was necessary to add eleven more steps. How is it possible to know pride in the face of such wonder?

In his epiphany moment on the corner of Fourth and Walnut in Louisville, Kentucky, Thomas Merton saw the passersby in a new way. He wrote, "I saw the secret beauty of their hearts. . . . They are walking around shining like the sun." And he concluded, rather wistfully, that if we could see others and ourselves that way, "I suppose the big problem would be that we would fall down and worship each other."

Old Monk is starting to realize that it's not only other people before whom she should prostrate. It's all of creation that must be looked at with new eyes. She must become more like Rev. Eido Tai Shimano, who writes:

People often ask me how Buddhists answer the question: "Does God exist?" The other day I was walking along the river. . . . I was suddenly aware of the sun, shining through the bare trees. Its warmth, its brightness, and all this completely free, completely gratuitous. Simply there for us to enjoy. And without my knowing it, completely spontaneously, my two hands came together, and I realized that I was making gassho [praying hands]. And it occurred to me that this is all that matters: that we can bow, take a deep bow. Just that. Just that.

Old Monk looks forward to the day when, she too, approaches all people, all creation in the posture of a profound bow.

CR

Resisting War's Madness

Old Monk is in conflict on holidays like Memorial Day and July 4. She believes that war is wrong under all circumstances and that, especially in this day of possible nuclear annihilation and drone madness, it is morally indefensible. But veterans are another matter. Old Monk can't stomach the hypocrisy in politics and media where soldiers are praised and lauded for defending freedom and everyone applauds and raises flags and feels so patriotic . . . until, until these young soldiers come home from war.

If they come home dead, there is fitting tribute. But if they come home broken in body and soul, a great silence descends. There's only silence while they seek mental help to erase the nightmares of deeds done or witnessed in Iraq or Afghanistan. Only silence while they roam the streets searching for a place to sleep. Only silence while they stand in soup kitchen lines. Only silence when they're thrown in jail for drug or violent crimes. Only silence while their families disintegrate because "this isn't the same person I knew before they went to war." Only silence while the suicides pile up in record numbers.

What can we do for these young women and men who may have been filled with the highest ideals and a heroic sense of self-giving when they put on a uniform? First, we can stop war. We can stop romanticizing and glamorizing it. We can stop declaring it and participating in it. There are alternative ways to fight for justice and peace. The elimination of war is our great gift to its survivors.

Then we must do everything possible to ensure that these present victims of war don't spend the rest of their lives in virtual body bags. As much money as was allocated to the war must be designated to assisting its veterans. Their needs must become a top budget priority, allocating monies for high-caliber outreach programs, clinics, hospitals, counselors, psychiatrists, homes, and so on. And all of us should look for concrete ways to become a compassionate presence in at least one veteran's life.

And lastly, on Memorial Day we should also pay tribute to all who resist war's madness. All the conscientious objectors and dissenters who said "no" and took the consequences of jail, work camps, society's scorn, and rejection.

ॐ

When Walls Disappear

Old Monk often wonders how many people really understand what we are trying to do at Monasteries of the Heart, what a radical experiment it is in monastic spirituality.

It's so gratifying, then, to receive a paper done by a doctoral student at Boston University outlining the revolutionary theory presented in both the book *The Monastery of the Heart: An Invitation to a Meaningful Life* by Joan Chittister and the movement itself.

Dr. Bin Song, who was lecturer of Western philosophy at Nankai University, China, and now is a PhD candidate in religious studies at Boston University, calls Monasteries of the Heart "cutting edge . . . a creative impulse to revive the [Benedictine] tradition in a startlingly innovative way." He understands that a main contribution being made by Monasteries of the Heart is "a new concept of community . . . a cyberspace monastery . . . which prioritizes the inheritance and transmission of Benedictine spirituality based upon the individual's spontaneity, group cooperation, and communal self-discipline over and above any physical or institutional manifestation of monastic life."

He outlines both the possibilities as well as the challenges that occur when the "walls" of the monastery disappear. He notes that a cyberspace monastery incarnates Benedict's dream that strangers be welcomed without prejudice or stereotype, but he also sees this acceptance without traditional formation and formal acceptance into community as our biggest challenge.

It's obvious that he has spent lots of time on our website because he cites our online forum to highlight the problem: "Radical equality, sometimes even in an anonymous way, engenders enormous differences among opinions. Then how to harmonize these different voices into a communal spiritual focus and to let the difference enrich rather than vitiate the spiritual pursuit will become a huge challenge for this new virtual monastery."

Old Monk agrees but also knows, based on over fifty years in a traditional monastery, that the problem of harmonizing differences and reaching consensus is not unique to a cyberspace monastery. It is certainly more obvious in an online monastery because every opinion is voiced for the world to read. Old Monk also agrees that more concrete ways need to be developed to unite members in a common effort that will, indeed, transform both the members and the world.

But Monasteries of the Heart is only three years old, a spiritual baby. And Old Monk's heart soared with renewed energy when she read the last sentence of Bin Song's review:

> For all religious scholars who are not only interested in the history of religions but also attentive to its going-on process, for all religionists in kinds of traditions who are aspiring for enlivening their own tradition in modern society, and for spiritual seekers who want to maintain the purest zeal for seeking God without much ascetic tendency toward the seething and simmering contemporary world, I recommend this prose poetry, beautifully written and with insuperably appealing spirituality.

CR

Not Always So

Awareness is a mystery to Old Monk. Every spiritual book she reads tells her that to be aware is to be enlightened.

Old Monk even pretends she understands this and writes articles and blogs as if she has integrated this insight. She quotes Thich Nhat Hanh: "When you are eating, eat. When you are washing the dishes, wash the dishes."

But Old Monk can never do this. When she washes the dishes, she's thinking about a new project or how to fix her golf swing, or what she'll have at the next meal. Or she worries about her godson who is suffering terribly with a mental illness. Or she wonders if she will find a subject for the next blog. She's still not convinced that blanking the mind to concentrate on drying a cup is akin to the beatitudes. It also confuses her. After you do the dishes, then do you concentrate on putting them on the shelf, then walking to the porch, then sitting on the swing? When are you supposed to think? If she did this all day, she would go completely mad.

And she also wonders that if you are aware you are washing the dishes, are you aware of that or are you aware of being aware?

Yes, Old Monk is on a low rung of spiritual development. That's why she laughed aloud at this story:

> A Zen master had been teaching his disciples the importance of awareness and mindfulness. When the students came down to breakfast the next morning, they found the Master eating breakfast and reading the paper. The students were scandalized and shouted out, "Master, didn't you teach us: When you are eating breakfast, eat breakfast. When you are reading a newspaper, read a newspaper?"
>
> And the Master replied, "Exactly. And when you are eating breakfast and reading the newspaper, eat breakfast and read the newspaper."

Gotta love those Zen teachings that are supposed to explode the mind and free one from all ego-centeredness, judgment, and certainties. To help free herself from thinking there is one true answer to anything, including enlightenment, Old Monk has this teaching of Zen master Suzuki taped on her study wall: The secret of Zen in two words: "not always so."

CR

One Mystical Moment

Old Monk's best friend, Sister Mary, just left for a private retreat at a retreat center that she went to frequently when she was younger. Oh, and did Old Monk mention that it's the place where Mary had some intense spiritual experiences?

For example, it was during a long-ago private retreat that, while sitting and looking at the Niagara River, she was filled with an all-encompassing white light. Though she knew where she was, she felt transported to another place. People she knew and loved began to appear and be engulfed in the light until gradually the penetrating light expanded inside her to encompass the entire world. For a long time afterward she would pray for people by putting them in the white light. She would sit still, visualize the person, and a piercing white light would appear, surrounding the person with comfort and love. The white light stayed with Mary for a long period of time and then disappeared.

"Are you hoping for another white light experience?" Old Monk asked her before she left. She just smiled.

Old Monk hasn't had many such spiritual highs. Maybe one. Hers occurred at the Metropolitan Museum of Art in New York City the first time she visited the Christmas angel tree. It, too, was a mystical moment that brought a sense of immeasurable joy and unity with the self and the universe.

Old Monk's tried to recapture that experience by returning to the Met three other times during the holiday season. No luck.

So, what is the purpose of these peak spiritual moments that are probably experienced by most ordinary people at least once in a lifetime? Do they occur when you need them most? Are they given as a taste of the Untastable? Are they given to sustain through the dry and dark periods?

౷

An Act of Kindness

A rather prominent woman in town bicycles twice a week around the Lake Erie peninsula. On one of her trips she noticed a disheveled, obviously homeless man sitting on one of the benches at the entrance of the state park.

"If he's still there when I'm on my way home, I going to buy him lunch," she said to herself.

An hour later and he still sat, staring at the water, and enjoying the sun. She stopped and asked, "Would you like an ice cream cone?"

"I'd like that very much," he answered.

She told him that she had to attach her bike to the car, and he should meet her at the ice cream and hot dog stand, a walk of about two or three blocks. When she arrived, he was waiting. She introduced herself as Barbara and shook his hand.

"I'm John," he said.

He smelled badly of urine, Barbara told me, so she was glad when he asked to sit in one of the outside tables to share a hot dog, soda, and ice-cream lunch. "A few moments into the conversation, I realized he was mentally ill, probably schizophrenic, but he had good table manners and was so polite and attentive that I knew he came from a good home," Barbara said. When it came time to leave, John grabbed her hands and thanked her for her kindness. Then he reached out and hugged her. "When I told my husband what happened, he had a fit and got angry," Barbara said. "He was worried about me, of course." But I said to him, "What if it were our son, Brady, who was sick and hungry and homeless? Wouldn't you want someone to show him an act of kindness?"

Old Monk can understand this. My godchild, a boy I raised since he was five years old, is thirty-two years old now. A week ago he left town. As I write this, he is in New York City somewhere. Penniless. Homeless. Old Monk's heart is broken. If you see him, don't be afraid. He's my boy. Offer him something to eat.

❧

Listening to Rain

A soft but steady rain falls here, and I'm reminded that, alone in his hermitage, Thomas Merton wrote a poetic essay on rain that included these words:

What a thing it is to sit absolutely alone, in the forest, at night, cherished by this wonderful, unintelligible, perfectly innocent speech, the most comforting speech in the world, the talk that rain makes by itself all over the ridges, and the talk of the watercourses everywhere in the hollows! Nobody started it, nobody is going to stop it. It will talk as long as it wants, this rain. As long as it talks, I am going to listen.

So today should be a day of listening. The truth is I am not very good at listening to nature. Maybe I'm not very good at listening, period. But I don't spend much time in nature. Oh, I was outside a lot growing up, but I never paid attention to bugs and blossoms and clouds. I don't know the names of wildflowers or trees or seashells or stones. I can't tell the difference between the morning song of a sparrow, a thrush, a robin, or a wren. I prefer to write of flowers and leaves and snowfall from inside, looking out my window. I have never been a friend of woods. I abhor camping because it's hard on my asthma. I can never find the Big Dipper. Sunrises and sunsets on Lake Erie are miracles, but I get my fill. Don't write me off as a complete nature loser, however. One thing I can't live without is water. Whenever I need to find inner peace, I recall hours spent sitting on a deck or beach or shoreline staring at Lake Douglas, Lake Findley, the Caribbean, Lake Erie.

Before I die, I want to change. I want to connect with the spiders, tree limbs, stars, moon phases, and mud. In fact, Old Monk is going out into the rain right now without an umbrella. She is going to sit in a chair in the yard and get soaking wet. And she's going to listen. On the other hand, Merton wrote his beautiful essay on rain listening to it from inside his cabin. And Merton has always been a mentor.

∾

A Few Minutes Each Day

"Do you think that's true?" I asked. "And, if it's true, who would those people be?"

I was asking the question of the four sisters who live on our inner-city block and gather to pray each morning. Sister Mary had just finished the daily reading from Sister Joan Chittister's *The Monastic Way,* and I was thinking aloud about it. This was the reading: "The power of the personality is one of the greatest powers on earth. Ask any government that has been overcome by a charismatic person without a sword."

"Lech Walesa in Poland." "Aung San Suu Kyi in Burma." "Mahatma Gandhi in India," were the first three responses. We talked a little bit more about the power of nonviolence in overthrowing oppressive governments and then finished prayer.

A short sharing after we read from *The Monastic Way* is not a daily occurrence, but it is a regular one. And so is the habit of my thinking about the quote during the rest of the day. I found myself going back over all those great figures who challenged unjust authority without a sword—Susan B. Anthony in the United States, Mairead Corrigan Maguire in Ireland, Maha Ghosananda in Cambodia, Martin Luther King Jr. in the United States, Rigoberta Menchú in Guatemala, Nelson Mandela in South Africa, Corazon Aquino in the Philippines, to name a few. It was a worthwhile spiritual practice that day.

Old Monk likes reading notes we get from readers of *The Monastic Way* who tell us how they use it. Most use it for daily personal reflection. Spouses discuss it over morning coffee. Small groups meet for monthly discussions around it. And men and women in prison post the readings on the walls of their cells, meet with chaplains to share ideas, and journal each day.

"Know thyself? If I knew myself, I'd run away," Johann Wolfgang Goethe wrote. Well, for many, a few minutes each day with *The Monastic Way* has gone a long way toward self-knowledge and self-acceptance. And that is a good work that Old Monk is proud to be a part of.

CR

Reinventing the Rosary

"Reader's Retreat with Joan Chittister" is an event that can't be described. It has to be experienced. Forty women came together this year to explore Joan's book *For Everything a Season*. Well, that's the starting point. What happens during the three days is part spiritual direction, part community-building, part party, and spiritual growth par excellence.

And, of course, there are the impassioned conversations that take place outside the scheduled sessions. One of my most sacred encounters during the retreat happened when Maureen sat down beside me and said, "I think you might be interested in how I say the rosary."

Maureen is a beautiful soul. She survived breast cancer, but recently it arrived again, this time with a vengeance. But Maureen doesn't let it stop her from being one of the kindest, most contemplative, life-affirming, and gentle people I know.

How she began praying to Mary is a story in itself. She told me that one night she parked her car in front of the church next door to her house in Brooklyn. When she got out of the car an intense ray of light leapt from the Mary statue that stood in front of the church and engulfed her. "I looked behind me to see if anyone was there, because I couldn't believe this light was meant for me," she told me. "I said to myself, 'You hate the Catholic Church. You make jokes about Mary. This light can't be meant for you.' But I couldn't deny it. The light was all encompassing."

She took the experience as a personal invitation to return to her roots, not with the faith of her childhood but with the spirituality of the new Maureen. One of the old traditions that she reexamined was the rosary.

"Since all religious traditions use some type of beads and the rosary has been so important to so many, I went to a talk on the rosary at our parish church to see if I could learn anything that would make sense to me." The presenter spoke about the first three beads on the rosary as dedicated to the Trinity. Maureen asked herself, "Who is the trinity in my life?" And she answered: my mother, my father, and my grandmother. So, she prays those three beads this way, "Holy Mother, full of grace, God is with you, blessed are you among all women." And then she says a personal prayer to her mother. On the next bead, it's "Holy Father, full of grace." And on the third bead, "Holy Grandmother, full of grace."

On each of the fifty remaining beads she uses the same method to pray for a living family member or friend or neighbor. "I love praying the rosary this way," she told me. "I grab my beads when I have a few minutes during the day, and I go to sleep with the rosary slipping through my fingers."

Maureen told me that story on October 7, the feast of the Holy Rosary. Since the purpose of the rosary is to reverence all the mysteries of our life—the times of friendship, betrayal, new birth, agony—Old Monk thinks Maureen has found a unique and profound way to honor her life's journey into God.

ॐ

The Bell Ringer

A poem by an anonymous author states:

> After the monastery bell fell and cracked,
> The valley seemed at once to know:
> How often its sound in the fresh dawn, the intimate twilight
> Had called out: "Awaken! Awaken!
> Remember! Remember!"
> It stopped at one's chest and entered in.

As a novice I was the monastery bell ringer. Seven times a day I pulled the bell rope to summon the community to prayer. Seven times a day the bell sounded through the lower east side of the city where the monastery was located and announced the sacredness of time, reminding neighbors to pause and remember why they were rocking the baby or baking a peach pie or washing the windows. The ringing of the bells and the pause of great silence that followed, bathed the ordinary in the holy. If given a choice, bell ringer is a calling Old Monk would have embraced.

Now, Old Monk sits in her inner-city study and listens to the neighborhood church bells. Because it's the inner city, the bells can ring every hour from 6 a.m. to nightfall—no one living here has enough clout to call city hall and have them stopped as a nuisance or disturber of sleep. Thank God.

In the gun-riddled area that now surrounds the once middle-class ethnic parish, church bells remind Old Monk to "awaken" and "remember" why she is here. Old Monk is here as a reminder that each life in this neighborhood, no matter how battered and pain-riddled and lonely and rejected, is precious. Listen. The church bells are ringing. May these bells continue to touch Old Monk's heart and enter in.

ॐ

Nothing More Beautiful

Autumn is my favorite season, but I used to worry because I liked the sadness that settled inside me when the fullness of flowers and fields and trees gradually peeled away to the barren. "Is there something wrong with me," I wondered, "that I look forward to the melancholy of fall?" Then I read a quote from Henry David Thoreau who said, "There is a certain fertile sadness which I would not avoid, but rather earnestly seek. It's a kind of contentment with the poignant and passing parts of life, rather than the surface of all sunshine."

Ah, Thoreau and me. Not bad company.

My attraction to "fertile sadness" also explains why I like the Japanese form of poetry called haiku. The haiku connects something in nature and one tiny moment of time taken from your life. In Japanese the poem usually consists of seventeen syllables in three phrases. When written in English its three brief lines, ten words or so, are about one breath long. "A haiku brings us the birth and death of each moment," writes poet-translator Patricia Donegan. And she goes on to explain that it is this awareness, acceptance, and appreciation of impermanence, of the transient, reflected especially in nature, that the Japanese call "sad beauty."

There it is—"sad beauty." I find nothing more beautiful than drying corn stalks, one last red leaf on a tree branch, field crickets crying under a harvest moon, a lone loon fading into mist.

In autumn especially Old Monk is reminded that everything tends to vanish. And that fills her with tender sadness and reminds her to make every moment more precious still.

> in large rain puddle
> dozens of yellow leaves
> one pink rose petal
> autumn rain—
> only my pen to fight
> the dying light.

CR

Dipa Ma

I'm always pleased when I'm introduced to a woman saint that I haven't met before. Recently I read a book about Dipa Ma, a Buddhist master, described by one of her students this way: "I was able to rest in her silence, like resting under a large shade tree." What a lovely image for a spiritual teacher.

Like most Indian girls of her time, Dipa Ma was given in marriage at the age of twelve to a man twenty-five-years-old. Over the years they grew to love one another and had one child, a daughter. When Dipa Ma was in her forties, her beloved husband died, and she decided to follow a call that had haunted her since youth. Dipa Ma wanted to learn to meditate. It wasn't long before her unusual spiritual gifts were recognized, and people began flocking to her. Rather than rooting herself in a temple or monastery, she taught meditation right from her home in the heart of Calcutta while keeping a normal housekeeping schedule. As word of her holiness spread, people flocked to her small apartment, both neighbors and seekers from abroad. Included in these seekers were Sharon Salzberg, Joseph Goldstein, and Jack Kornfield, three of the leading figures of Buddhism in the United States. It is no exaggeration to say that Dipa Ma greatly influenced Buddhist meditation in the West.

It's no secret that most women saints celebrated in Western Christianity are either nuns or martyrs who died preserving their virginity. The same holds true of Buddhist masters—rare, rare indeed, is a laywoman Buddhist master. That's why Old Monk is so happy to find Dipa Ma.

An excerpt from the book *Dipa Ma: The Life and Legacy of a Buddhist Master* by Amy Schmidt that Old Monk copied was from a group interview:

> Jack Kornfield asked Dipa Ma, "What is it like in your mind?" Dipa Ma smiled, closed her eyes, and quietly answered, "In my mind there are three things: concentration, loving-kindness, and peace."

Old Monk wonders how she would answer that question.

⚘

Party with Your Thoughts

I like to read books on meditation, but I've never gotten into watching my breath go in and out or repeating a sacred word for thirty minutes. God knows I've tried . . . and failed. A psychiatrist would have a field day with me. Every time I try to be mindful of my breathing, I almost hyperventilate. I think it has something to do with having asthma and the fear of dying while gasping for breath. Or perhaps it's some suppressed childhood trauma. Or maybe it's just not my path.

So I've come to peace with the fact that I meditate best with a pen. I realize it's a minor meditation level, and I probably will never observe or extinguish the ten knots or obstructions to enlightenment that master Dipa Ma described, but it's home to me.

The Persian poet Hafiz once wrote: "Who would want to live with some crickets in your room carousing loudly all night? That is to say, either befriend all your thoughts, party with them the best you can . . . or toss the rascals out."

Old Monk likes to party with her thoughts rather than follow the meditation instruction to recognize the thought, let it go, and return to awareness of her breath. Indeed, the best hour of Old Monk's day is spent carousing with her crickets, a sheet of paper, and a pen. The sixty-minute party is usually exhausting but soul stretching. And on rare occasions—if Old Monk is lucky—a sliver of enlightenment might slip in.

ल्ड

Watering a Dead Stick

Here's a Desert Wisdom story that's gone through a lot of abuse:

Abba John the Dwarf was commanded by his superior to stick a dry stick into the ground and water it until it bore fruit. For three years Abba John watered it twice a day with water that he drew from a river two miles away. At the end of three years the wood came to life and bore fruit. Then Abba John carried some of the fruit to prayer and shared it with the community saying, "Take and eat the fruit of obedience."

Prior to Vatican II this story was used to beat religious into blind obedience. Sisters were told to do mundane and senseless things under the guise of holy obedience and forbidden to question anything—just keep watering that dry wood. Why? Because the superior said so, that's why. With Vatican II, the story of watering a dead stick became a joke and disappeared from any instruction.

But Old Monk got thinking about it again when she received an email from Benedictines for Peace Erie reminding her to attend the monthly vigil being held "until the Immigration Law is passed." Given that people have been gathering once a month for a year now, writing countless letters, signing endless petitions, and given the results of the November national election . . . is Old Monk the only one who feels like this is watering a dry stick?

And yet, though Old Monk was unable to go in November, she plans to be there next month. So what's the difference? The difference is that maybe Old Monk didn't look closely enough at the Desert Story. Maybe the point of the story isn't necessarily what happened to the dry stick but what happened to the one who watered it day after day in search of good fruit. Maybe the point of the story is bringing forth new life by being faithful to a call. In other words, what if the dry wood was Abba John himself? And maybe after three years of faithfulness to a spiritual practice, Abba John blossomed anew.

So Old Monk will join a handful of others on a dark street corner in cold temperatures, snow flying everywhere, because standing in vigil for justice is a contemporary spiritual practice. And, along with the others who are much more faithful than Old Monk, she will repeat the spiritual practice over and over again. Though it may appear as futile as watering dead wood, Old Monk trusts that even dry lands can bloom and bring forth flowers. She hopes it might happen in the desert of Congress; she is certain it can occur in the wasteland of her own heart.

CR

Blessing Ritual

The Cleveland Clinic is not a place where I would have chosen to travel to on my Advent journey. But here I am to stand watch with Sister Joan as she undergoes complex abdominal surgery. It was comforting to read in the scriptures today, "God will wipe away the tears from all faces." And yet I pray the words knowing it is we who must banish or at least reduce the weeping of the world. In this huge hospital complex alone there is enough pain to drown the universe with tears. To imagine the tears of the suffering world— the hunger, the torture, the maiming of war, let alone the personal anguish—is too much to comprehend. "Behold, God comes to save the people," the scripture proclaims. And I respond:

Jesus, read the headlines
the little children need you
to come unto them

The four community members who are here with Sister Joan gathered around her hospital bed before the surgery and performed a blessing ritual using two vials of healing liquids Joan had brought with her. First, we broke open the seal of Saint Walburga oil and each of us took a turn blessing her forehead, her hands, her stomach area. Then we repeated the gestures with water from the healing well of Saint Brigid of Kildare from the other vial.

Once a year liquid seeps from the tomb of Saint Walburga, whose remains are in a German monastery that bears her name in Eichstätt, Bavaria, the home of origin of the Benedictine Sisters of Erie. The liquid is known as Saint Walburga's oil and has been used for centuries as a healing agent. Joan recalled how our Sister Theophane, a nurse, used to rub Joan's legs with the oil when she was stricken with polio as a teenager. And the waters of Brigid go back thousands of years to the time when Brigid was worshiped as a Celtic goddess and later morphed into a Roman Catholic saint bearing the same name.

What really made it a healing service, of course, was the love extended to Joan by the four sisters gathered around her bedside who represented the hundreds of community members and friends praying for her at the same time. Lots of money is going into the marketing of healing therapy these days, but nothing has the power of love and friendship. Sitting up in bed now, Joan would agree.

❧

Get Real, Old Monk

> all my life
> men around a boardroom table
> deciding my fate

The *National Catholic Reporter* just announced that the report of the Vatican's apostolic visitation to women religious in the United States will be released December 16. Observers are hopeful because it is being released at an unprecedented news conference where religious representatives, including the president of the Leadership Conference of Women Religious, will be present. They point out that the two prelates previously in charge of the Congregation for Institutes of Consecrated Life and Societies of Apostolic Life have left their posts and been replaced by bishops seen as "friendlier toward women religious." I can get swept up in this "hope." Then I shake myself and say, "Get real, Old Monk." Do you know what the ratio of women religious is to priests in the world? In 2012 there were 700,000 women religious as compared to 400,000 priests. And who's in charge of our lives? Who makes all the decisions? Priests who become bishops, that's who. Bishops who become cardinals, that's who. Cardinals who become pope, that's who. Men. Men. Everywhere men. Even if the report is favorable, it is still a travesty.

More than ever, I need to keep praying today's responsorial psalm:

> There is one thing I ask of you;
> for this I long:
> to live in your house
> all the days of my life. (Ps 27:4)

☙

Mozart and Patti Smith

Jesus says, "Without cost you have received; without cost you are to give" (Mt 10:8). My companions today are two men who understood this. It's the feast of Saint Nicholas and the death anniversary of Wolfgang Amadeus Mozart. Though I love the legendary kindness of Bishop Saint Nick, I am more attracted to Mozart. Musicians, poets, and artists speak more deeply to me than theologians or bishops or leaders of revolutions. And this child prodigy and genius composer who died in abject poverty gave more to humanity than can be measured by his prodigious outpouring of music. Theologian Karl Barth, who played Mozart every morning before going to work on his dogma, said that "it is a child, even a 'divine' child who speaks in Mozart's music to us," and George Bernard Shaw wrote that Mozart's music is "the only music that would not sound out of place in the mouth of God."

> late November—
> on bare branch one bird
> still sings

A friend emailed me a video of Patti Smith singing "O Holy Night" at the 2013 Vatican Christmas Concert. What? Of all good things that I've read about Pope Francis, this gives me the most hope. Imagine the godmother of punk rock, as she is often called, even getting an invitation. But here's the thing—Patti Smith is a poet, author, Rock & Roll Hall of Famer, and one of our purest living souls. A few years ago I read her memoir, *Just Kids*, and was blown away by her honesty and the simple beauty of her prose. The book, which traces her relationship with photographer Robert Mapplethorpe during the 1960s and 1970s, won the 2010 National Book Award for Nonfiction.

ଔ

Benedictine Examen

Abba Poemen said of Abba Pior, "Every day he made a fresh beginning." And January 1 is like the feast day of fresh beginnings. My new calendar is hung, and my new books are selected. For my morning reading I like to keep four books running—a poetry book, a writing book, a "spiritual" book, and a daily shot-in-the-arm book. So, this morning I started *Blue Horses* by Mary Oliver, a Christmas present that I requested; *Pastrix: The Cranky, Beautiful Faith of a Sinner and Saint* by Nadia Bolz-Weber, a book recommended by a Monasteries of the Heart member; *Global Chorus: 365 Voices on the Future of the Planet*, edited by Todd E. MacLean. My writing book is *Publishing: A Writer's Memoir* by Gail Godwin, but it won't be available until January 13. Every day I read a small section from each book and so get through a couple dozen books a year this way. I also read about the saint of the day and daily scripture reflection from the monthly booklet *Give Us This Day*, published by Liturgical Press. Well, I sort of skim the reflections but spend a lot of time on the short saint biographies prepared by Robert Ellsberg.

And, of course, I started Journal 2015 this morning. At a recent funeral liturgy for one of our sisters, a community member gave a moving homily, using sections from the deceased sister's journal to highlight her spirituality. The raw, honest, and heartfelt words she put in her journal were a beautiful benchmark of her personal relationship with God. I sat in the pew wishing more sisters would keep a spiritual journal, and that we would devise a way to honestly share them. We would know each other on a much deeper level.

One spiritual practice that I don't do in a deliberate fashion anymore is a daily examen. Prior to Vatican II, we were expected to spend twenty minutes going over our day and listing all our faults and sins with the intent of amending. I found that practice negative and stopped doing it formally when it was no longer required, though I believe self-examination is what nudges conversion. What if I used the small space allotted in my five-year journal—enough for about three sentences a day—for a daily examen?

I've heard about two daily examens that I'm more attracted to. One is the Jesuit method practiced by Saint Ignatius of Loyola. Each night you ask yourself: "What was the most life-giving moment of the day? What was the most life-draining moment?" Another is practiced by a friend who told me that she closes the day by asking herself: "To whom was I kind today? To whom was I unkind?"

So, is there a Benedictine daily examen method? What if Old Monk reflected on Dom André Louf's question "What is a monk?" in light of the day's events? Maybe each day of my five-year journal would have only two sentences. In one sentence I would write when I think I acted like a monk that day. And in the other sentence, when I didn't. For example:

A monk is someone who stops for a moment and prays with the falling snow.

A monk is someone who wouldn't get sarcastic and roll her eyes at a staff meeting.

Now that kind of a five-year journal might be worth keeping.

CR

Daily Saints

Every morning, as I mentioned earlier, I read a short biography of a saint in the monthly missal *Give Us This Day* and raise a toast to Robert Ellsberg, who writes these snapshots of the holy among us. What impresses me the most are all the stories of women who, despite many obstacles—forced marriages, tyrannical fathers, persecution, cultural taboos, and sexist barriers up the wazoo—found a way to devote themselves to God and to the poor and suffering. Centuries before Nike introduced the slogan "just do it," these women lived it.

I read page after page about women who knew a call and set their faces to the wind. Today it's Saint Angela of Foligno, a woman of wealth who lost her whole family to the plague, gave all she owned away, joined the Third Order of Saint Francis, attracted to herself a community of men and women, became a mystic, and with her companions cared for the sick and poor. Here's one of her quotes: "The earth is pregnant with God." Wouldn't that make a wonderful environmental rallying cry?

> a woman mystic wrote
> the earth is pregnant with God—
> we but the midwives.

CR

Beware of Fanaticism

I grabbed a book of prayers and poems this morning intent on finding something for a newsletter and the first selection I opened to was this on, attributed to the Prophet Mohammad:

> What actions are
> most excellent?

To gladden the heart
of a human being.
To feed the hungry.
To help the afflicted.
To lighten the sorrow
of the sorrowful.
To remove the wrongs
of the injured.
That person is the
most beloved of God
who does the most good
to God's creatures.

It's the day after the terrorist bloodbath in Paris, when two Islamic gunmen wielding assault rifles barged into the French satirical magazine *Charlie Hebdo* and executed twelve journalists and wounded eleven others. "*Allahu Akbar*" (God is great) the assassins shouted running to the getaway car, satisfied that they had avenged the political cartoonist's crime of lampooning the Prophet Mohammad.

How does this happen? How do followers of great spiritual leaders turn into methodical torturers and killers and believe the great prophets bless their evil deeds? Christians did the same in the Crusades and the Inquisition—all in the name of the God of love. Once again, I am reminded to beware of fanaticism no matter what costume it wears—holy robes, cardinal hats, camouflage uniforms, select scripture verses. Beware of those who swear they know the truth, the whole truth, and nothing but the truth, so help me God. And always be mindful of the warning from an anonymous Parisian who placed a bouquet of roses at the massacre site with a quote by the French philosopher Diderot, "There is only one step from fanaticism to barbarism."

 os

Holy Friendship

A nanda, the beloved disciple of the Buddha, once asked his
teacher about the place of friendship in the spiritual journey.
"Master, is friendship half of the spiritual life?" he inquired. And
the Buddha replied, "Nay, Ananda, friendship is the whole of the
spiritual life."

One person who would definitely agree with the Buddha is
Abbot Aelred of Rievaulx, the Cistercian saint whose feast we celebrate today. Saint Aelred made friendship the hallmark of monastic
life, calling the lifestyle "a school of love." His treatise *On Spiritual
Friendship* should be read and studied by anyone who desires a deep
spiritual relationship with another.

It's no secret that in the centuries following Saint Aelred, close
friendships were discouraged in monastic communities, in all religious life, really. Thank God those days are over. It's only when
someone loved me that I began to know that I was lovable. And
that made all the difference. Human love freed me to accept myself
and gave me a taste of God's unconditional love, not just for me but
for all creation. After that there was nothing to fear. The Buddha
gets no argument from Old Monk—soul-friendship is the whole
of the spiritual life.

os

Last Breath in the Monastery

M uch as I hate the thought of death, a monastery is a good
place to take the final breath. We had two sisters die this
week, both on the same day. Sister Audrey was gone in thirty-three
hours—she was at supper on Saturday, rushed to the hospital at
1 a.m. Sunday, on a ventilator by 11 a.m. when all systems began

shutting down, and dead Monday morning. Before pneumonia paid a visit, she was one of the healthiest women in the community: a vegetarian, at the YMCA three times a week, vibrant, full-time job. Sister Claire had just returned from a visit to her beloved mission in the Yucatán Peninsula, Mexico, where she had served for years, and was planning to resume her chaplaincy at Polk State Center. But her long-time shadow, cancer, had other plans. The suddenness of the deaths numbed us all.

Though both sisters died in the hospital—unusual for us, most die in the monastery—our community death rituals held fast. Sisters who were able gathered around the hospital bedside to sing hymns and pray aloud and bless the departing and weep. It's a deeply human and profoundly spiritual rite of passage and doctors and nurses at both hospitals were also moved to tears.

Though I will not yet permit death to be my friend, I do hope that when I must meet this "angel" the room will be filled with holy voices and a few tears attesting to a felt love. Not a bad way for death to lose its sting and fear to be no more.

CR

Prisoner of Hope

One of the books I'm reading this year is *Global Chorus*, a short reflection a day on the environmental crisis. By the end of the first week of January, I was sorry that I bought the book. It seemed like one brief talk after another about how badly the earth was being treated and how we had to stop the abuse. "I can't take a year of preaching on the same theme," Old Monk said to herself. But today, at the end of the first month of readings, I have a different take. Now I look forward to reading how a few of the famous—Jane Goodall, Robert Bateman, Desmond Tutu—but mostly ordinary folk in every walk of life, are adding their brilliant notes to the global chorus.

"I am a prisoner of hope," wrote Desmond Tutu. When I'm lucky, I find myself locked in that prison, too. Unfortunately, I have an escape key in my pocket and use it too often—as when I click on the CNN app and read the headlines. Then I become a prisoner of doubt or despair or depression or anger or a handful of other negative emotions. Reading *Global Chorus* facilitates my return to the prison of hope. That's why it's so important for all of us to share our good works with one another, not out of any sense of pride but because the global chorus of hope needs to go viral. Old Monk's only desire is to be a "prisoner of hope," so she is looking forward to eleven more months of creative ideas on how to save the planet.

☙

Love in Action

Today I reread all the quotes and passages that I copied in my commonplace book during January. My favorite was voiced by one of those pioneer nineteenth-century nuns, Mother Joseph of the Sacred Heart, who left in her wake eleven hospitals, seven academies, and was inducted into the National Cowgirl Hall of Fame! She wrote:

> My dear sisters, allow me to recommend to you the care of the poor in our houses, as well as those without. Take good care of them; have no fear of them; assist them and receive them. Do not say: ah! this does not concern me, let others see to them. My sisters, whatever concerns the poor is always our affair.

Easier said than done. I heard recently that a new volunteer at the soup kitchen was complaining about the guests—the poor weren't what he expected. The trouble begins when volunteers imagine they will dish out food to lines of passive poor who smile politely and say, "Thank you," over and over again. So it's a shock when you dish out potatoes to a twenty-year-old who is wired to an iPhone and obviously on drugs, or a homeless person suffering from mental illness who swears at you, or a young single mother with four undisciplined children who is expecting a fifth. Then the judgments start.

Anytime I'm tempted to judge those who stand in line for a meal or a bed, I take out my tattered copy of a prayer by Saint Vincent de Paul. In that prayer Vincent warns do-gooders like me that the poor are really our masters, and the more demanding they seem, the more unjust and bitter, the more love you must give them. Why? "It is only because of your love," Vincent writes, "only because of your love that the poor will forgive you the food that you give them." Or I recall Dorothy Day's favorite quote from Dostoyevsky: "Love in action is a harsh and dreadful thing compared to love in dreams." And recently Old Monk read a lovely passage by Saint Augustine reminding that our Christian responsibility is not to decide who deserves help or doesn't, but to freely give alms and offer hospitality to all who ask. Augustine concludes, "You cannot be a judge and sifter of hearts."

Old Monk will leave the judging and sifting of hearts to God. In the meantime, Old Monk thanks God for the bounty she has been given—all of it undeserved—and will try to repay in kind.

CR

Listen to Women

It makes me smile when people tell me that I'm not in touch with "average" women when it comes to the issue of women and the church. They insist that most women in the pew are not upset over this issue, and it's only the concern of a small and vocal fringe group in the United States. Then I watch the extraordinary meeting that took place inside the Vatican on March 8, 2015, International Women's Day, and listen to women from around the globe address justice issues for women in church and society.

Then I get notes like this one from an "ordinary go-to-church-every-Sunday, parish-centered woman" and ask myself: who's really out of touch? The woman writes:

> Like you, I have had tough sledding in our church when it comes to women. On the feast of the Holy Family, our second reading was the one from Paul about wives being subservient (my friend who goes to another church in town said that wasn't their reading that day), and the deacon who gave the sermon said he didn't understand why those words offend some people, because it's really about wives and husbands loving each other. Then the same guy gave the sermon two weeks ago about the reading where Abraham is asked to sacrifice his son. I told the priest ahead of time that anyone who has lost a child cannot hear those words and think that God would ask that. Then I decided to just leave mass and go to try to watch the bald eagles at the South Pier instead. I couldn't find the eagles, but I know my head was clearer! I guess we've reached an age where we know what our intellects and intuition know about life and God and spirituality.

CR

What Is a Monk?

Since I didn't have any specific practice for Lent this year, I decided to use this question by Cistercian monk Dom André Louf as a daily prompt for forty days: "What is a monk?"

Here are a few of my answers to the question: What is a monk?

> a monk
> is someone who doubts
> every line in the creed
> but keeps it a secret
> even from herself.

a monk
is someone who paces
airports when delays are announced
as if she had
somewhere to be.

a monk
is someone who plans
the breakfast menu
during meditation—
one flavor at a time.

a monk
is someone who has insomnia,
pacing the hardwood floors,
fingering beads—
monkey mind unleashed.

a monk
is someone who fears
her robe will loosen
all blemishes naked
to the passing eye.

a monk
is someone who crawls
snail-like toward enlightenment
not certain she wants to see
with the eyes of God.

a monk
is someone who longs
to be free of the expectations
she has engraved in her heart
of what a monk is.

a monk
is someone who welcomes
the morning star, cloud hidden or clear:
"This is the day our God has made,
let us be glad and rejoice."

༒

Haiti's Palm Procession

As we enter into Palm Sunday, I am reminded of the one time
in my life when I really experienced what this holy day is
all about. It was December 1990, and I was in Haiti as part of a
Pax Christi USA delegation to help monitor the country's first
democratic presidential election. The international community was
involved because the previous year the military had opened fire on
those who were brave enough to try to cast a ballot, and elections
were aborted.

It was quite an election day, with the poor trudging miles by foot
to vote, all of them putting their lives at risk since no one knew
how the military would react. Most of the people couldn't read, so
they voted by dipping their thumb in ink and marking the symbol
of a political candidate.

When the voting closed, the four women observers from Pax
Christi USA and election officials from Jacmel, the town where
we were monitoring, were locked in an abandoned and dilapi-
dated school building by the military so we could tabulate votes.
We watched as the Haitian officials counted paper ballots aloud by
candlelight and by the beam of the battery-charged video camera
carried by one of our members—no electricity, of course. The
Rooster ballot, the symbol of Jean-Bertrand Aristide, the former
Haitian priest who had been an outspoken advocate for justice and
now symbolized all the hope of Haiti's oppressed poor for liberation,
won the election in Jacmel by overwhelming numbers.

The ballot boxes were hoisted on small trucks and from across Haiti the procession began as truck after truck made its way into the capital of Port-au-Prince for the final tabulation. We followed the trucks from Jacmel to ensure the safety of the votes, and it was in this procession that I experienced Palm Sunday. As we neared the capital, hordes of people lined the roads, waving large palm branches and singing. "Hosanna," the three million people of Port-au-Prince shouted to the approaching trucks and vans of international observers. Even though the final election results were not yet announced, the poor of Haiti believed that their "savior" was arriving in those ballot boxes and they would finally be freed from oppression.

Yes, Aristide won in a landslide, and the poorest country in the Western Hemisphere erupted into delirious joy echoing the words of Martin Luther King Jr.: "Free at last, free at last, thank God Almighty we are free at last." Well, the overwhelming majority of the Haitian people sang that song. The wealthy elite and countries like the United States who couldn't stomach another socialist country in the hemisphere made sure the euphoria was short lived. Aristide was ousted by a coup and on the run in a matter of months. But there was that Palm Sunday moment that the people of Haiti and of Jerusalem experienced. And we recreate it every year, too—a Savior is coming on a donkey to free us and bring justice and peace. It is enough to sustain us in the struggle.

CR

Bomb Train Vigils

Today I joined a few dozen others in a vigil in front of the Federal Court House to draw attention to the thirty-two "bomb" trains that pass through my hometown each week. It was also the two-year anniversary of the train explosion in Lac-Mégantic, Canada, that incinerated forty-seven innocent civilians when one of the trains derailed. I was quite ignorant of the fact that each of the trains chugging through Erie has one-hundred tank cars containing thirty-thousand gallons of highly combustible crude oil. I also found out that the oil containers were not built to carry this kind of material and easily split open on contact. Even more disturbing is that in 2009 there were ninety-five-hundred tanker cars transporting crude oil across the United States, and in 2015 there are half a million, resulting in more frequent derailments.

While we were at the vigil, an ambulance, siren screaming, sped by toward some emergency. I tried to imagine what the noise level would be if a bomb-train disaster happened here and every available ambulance, fire engine, and police car in the county were summoned. What chaos would ensue, because no urban area is prepared to deal with an explosion of this magnitude.

Standing at the protest vigil yesterday, I was again tempted to give in to futility. All the same faces, only different posters. Sometimes it's "Close Guantanamo" or "Immigration Reform Now" or "Stop Fracking" or "No to War." Today it's "Ban 'Bomb' Trains." Yes, I know, we are called to be faithful, not successful. But still, isn't this a colossal waste of time?

I'm just finishing *The Way of the Dreamcatcher: Spirit Lessons with Robert Lax* by S. T. Georgiou. The book is a series of conversations that took place over many years between the poet Lax, who lived as a hermit on a Greek island, and Steve Georgiou, a young seeker who visited him.

In the section of the book that I read today a big fly enters Lax's house, and Georgiou—who has been trained by Lax—goes to find a plastic cup to capture the insect and set it free. He asks Lax why he goes to such extremes to save ants, spiders, even cockroaches. He notes that Lax walks along roads very carefully so that he doesn't step on even the tiniest creature. "You don't even step on cut flowers you find in the road," Georgiou writes. "Instead, you place them off to the side." And Lax replies, "All creatures are my friends, and all creatures hate pain. . . . Nothing dies. Maybe if we acted like nothing were dead, but rather alive and highly sensitive, we might become more gentle."

I am not at that stage of enlightenment. I trap and kill mice and squash spiders and swat flies and call the exterminator for roaches. But I do believe that Lax is right, and I yearn for such pure goodness. The bomb-train connection came after Georgiou caught the fly and released it to the open sky. Lax said to him: "Now didn't that make you happy? Isn't that what lasting happiness is all about? You had the choice to kill or save, and you saved. You gave life."

That's why a bomb-train vigil—or any protest against injustice and violence—is not a waste of time. It's always a choice between life and death. And to choose life is what lasting happiness is always about.

> on the overpass—
> a train of oil tanker "bombs"
> many wild flowers

CR

Mercy Is Always the Message

Last week I went to hear Kathy, a Monasteries of the Heart member, give a talk on Thomas Merton at her church. Kathy used one of Merton's quotes for her title, "God is mercy within mercy within mercy."

To start the talk, Kathy asked the audience what the word *mercy* meant to them. "Loving kindness," a woman offered. "Forgiveness," another said. "Compassion," a man suggested. Kathy listened to the responses and began, "Mercy is radical," when a woman interrupted her. "I know what mercy is," the woman said. "It's what the Benedictine sisters did this week after someone set fire to their soup kitchen. The sisters said that the man who started the fire ate at the Emmaus Soup Kitchen and so was part of the Emmaus family. They said they hoped he got help and was always welcome back. That's what I think mercy is."

Sister Mary Miller, the director of Emmaus Ministries, was the one facing the cameras after the fire. She is also my best friend. So, we've been talking a lot about the incident this past week. "If someone had been injured or killed in the fire (three sisters lived above the soup kitchen), I certainly would have different feelings," she said to me one day, "but the message wouldn't change. I might have to deal with feelings of deep anger and a desire for revenge, but mercy is always the message."

In her talk Kathy used the image of nesting dolls to try to comprehend what it means to say "God is mercy within mercy within mercy." A merciful heart is created in layers until you reach the core of unconditional love.

And how does one reach that core? Here's one way, from the desert monastics: "Sit in your cell and your cell will teach you everything."

Recently I learned a bit more about its author, Saint Moses the Black or, as he is more commonly called, Abba Moses. Seems he had been an Ethiopian servant or slave who was let go because of his thievery, and then he became the leader of a ruthless gang. He was converted by Christian monks while fleeing the law and became a great spiritual master. Abba Moses is a good example of why it's important to sin boldly. People who sin boldly, express contrition, and remember their past are always the most compassionate. They cannot judge another human being's failings because they know themselves too well. There is this story about him:

Abba Moses was called to a meeting to discuss the punishment of an errant monk. He picked up a basket with holes and filled it with sand and set out. As he walked, the sand left a trail behind him. Asked to explain himself he said, "My sins run out behind me and I do not see them, but today I am coming to judge the errors of another?"

CR

I Want to Be Surprised

On the way to a fall outdoor festival with a couple friends, we passed a cemetery and saw another friend of ours at the graveside of her recently deceased husband. Of course we stopped and shared hugs and tears. The widow pressed me about the afterlife, and all I could say was, "I want to be surprised."

I've made my peace with death. But I don't live for what happens beyond the grave. I only want to cherish the gratuitous, simple, and surprising gifts of the moment like the first bite of a tomato fresh from the garden or the fields of yellow cornstalks against the cloudless blue sky or the crow balancing itself on the top branch of a bare tree. Everything is so precious and beautiful and fleeting. I am sitting here right now almost in tears because of how the morning sunlight falls on a vase in my study. I am reminded of Mary Oliver's lines,

> Oh, to love what is lovely, and will not last!
> What a task
> to ask
> of anything, or anyone,
> yet it is ours,
> and not by the century or the year, but by the
>   hours.

I suppose that at one time I was motivated to do good because of a promise of future reward, but that left long ago. Now I try to do good because . . . well, because that's all you can do in return for the privilege of being able to "love what is lovely, and will not last." I just want to develop a deeper desire to nourish and protect and love all that exists here on earth as it is in heaven for tomorrow's children.

CR

Face of Mary

geese head south
pulling out giant sunflowers
by the roots

Since we are in the Year of Mercy proclaimed by Pope Francis, I am trying to pay attention to acts of mercy being performed by others. Hoping, of course, that I become a bit more merciful. As I mentioned earlier, my best friend, Sister Mary Miller, is the director of our soup kitchen, so I have an advantage when it comes to watching acts of mercy. Here's what I witnessed today:

Early this morning I went to the bus station with Mary. She was meeting a young man who was at the soup kitchen yesterday and asked her to help him get to Harrisburg, Pennsylvania. "I'm homeless and afraid," he said. "What's in Harrisburg?" she asked the slightly built teenager who has a right to be afraid in any shelter. "My grandfather," he said. All these young men and women roaming our city streets, nomads in the modern desert, searching for a friendly oasis to get a bit of rest and warmth. At least for two hours a day the Emmaus Soup Kitchen is an oasis of sorts.

The young man didn't show, so Mary left the ticket money with one of three soup-kitchen regulars who were waiting at the bus station until the public library opened. It was a cold day and, forced out of the overnight shelter at 7:00 a.m., they go to the Greyhound terminal for warmth until they can find refuge in the library. "You can trust me, Sister Mary," the man said, taking her $76. "And I can," she told me.

In the afternoon Mary got a letter from the man who is in prison being charged with setting fire to the soup kitchen. He has been sending her letters regularly. Again, he apologized and told her it was a 100 percent accident. "I always have and continue to keep up on the Emmaus Soup Kitchen news," he wrote, and enclosed two articles about Emmaus that he had ripped out of the Erie newspaper. His trial is coming up and "I hope you will show up to speak on my behalf."

"If it's possible, I will," Mary said. "He's a good man with a lot of problems."

See, three acts of mercy for me to imitate. Probably the one that meant the most was how naturally Mary handed the soup-kitchen regular $76 and trusted that he would give it to the boy if he showed up or return it to her at the soup kitchen if he didn't. How many people would do that? In this instance, she fed the hungry with a sense of dignity and friendship.

☙

Retreat Questions

I've made fifty-seven annual retreats with the Benedictine Sister of Erie. Of those, about half a dozen are memorable. But I'd place this year's June retreat, led by Mauritius Wilde, OSB, a monk from Christ the King Priory, Schuyler, Nebraska, in the top five. He presented some very unique and creative insights into the life of Benedict that surprised and engaged me. There is so little original literature on Saint Benedict—just the *Dialogues of Saint Gregory* and the Rule of Saint Benedict—that after fifty plus years, you think you've heard all the exegesis possible. But his take on the *Dialogues* was refreshing, tracing Benedict's journey as an archetype for each person's spiritual development, toward detachment from father, mother, spiritual fixations, sexuality, church, culture, power, and control.

He also did a great exercise with us on faith sharing. He had each of us think of the first part of two questions dealing with religion, community, faith, meaning—important topics. For example: In twenty years I think the church will. . . . If I had a chance to talk with Saint Benedict, I'd ask him. . . .

Then he asked for two volunteers. Two sisters sat facing each other: One spoke her part of the statement, and the other answered. Then they reversed roles. He repeated the exercise with three sets of volunteers. The purpose was to show that each of us—no matter our educational background or life experiences—has questions and beliefs to share, and we should risk voicing them. He pointed out that to evangelize is to ask questions, to make yourself vulnerable, to tell the truth, to risk. This is what draws people to the spiritual journey.

I remember a number of questions, and my own, too: The part of the Apostle's Creed that means the most to me is. . . . I think a monk is. . . .

As far as the public exchange goes, I've been thinking about one phrase that Sister Anne voiced. She said, "A major life event that I would like to design a ritual for is . . ." I would complete that phrase with two major life events: sisters' funerals and Holy Thursday. For both of these events it is not necessary for clergy to be present. Since the church gives the option of celebrating a funeral without a eucharistic liturgy, how could a community of women celebrate and bury one of its own? Since Holy Thursday is not a holy day of obligation, how could a community of women celebrate the memory of Jesus in the breaking of bread and sharing of wine?

One last thing. At the beginning of the retreat Mauritius invited us to change one small personal behavior or habit. If you're a reader, he said, go out and sit in nature instead. If you jump out of bed every morning at 5:30 a.m., stay in bed a little longer. If you pride yourself on fasting, eat a special treat. I decided not to pay attention to that. Myself, I rev up for retreats, getting a reading list and planning my schedule carefully. So what happened? I picked up a minor summer cold and slept for hours on end. For the most part, that was it—attend the lectures and sleep. Like I said, one of the best retreats of my life.

CR

Saved by That Which Ignores Us

I was pontificating before two young women about how writer and mystic Andrew Harvey was enlightened. I was telling them that he was in India visiting temple after temple in his mad pursuit of the divine when one day he got lost and found himself by a stream.

As he sat there, he noticed the way the sunlight had alighted on a few large rocks and . . . *Satori*—he was enlightened. He concluded that "we are saved by that which ignores us."

In other words, I said, it's when we realize the grandeur of all that was here before us and will remain long after we are gone; it's when we recognize how truly insignificant we are in the scheme of things; it's when we acknowledge that most of creation pays no attention to us at all that we recognize our humble place in the universe and in the heart of God. To find ourselves, we must forget ourselves.

On and on, I was going, loving the sound of my own voice.

Then I turned to Mary, my best friend, and said, "What do you think of that?" And she said, "I'm sorry, what did you say? I was ignoring you."

CR

To Be Rooted

"To be rooted is perhaps the most important and least recog- nized need of the human soul." I love this quote by Simone Weil and ruminate on it often. Most recently I saw it in action at a family funeral.

One of my nephews, Ted, spoke for the family at the memory service for his mother, my sister-in-law, who died young (sixty- seven years old) from Alzheimer's complications after ten long years of struggle. He asked his five siblings to send him a memory they wished to share.

My other nephew, John, shared this story. He told how his mother approached him one day and said, "I wonder if your brother is gay. He never brings home any girlfriends." "I knew what she was doing," John said. "She didn't want to put me on the spot by asking me directly if I was gay—maybe I wasn't ready to talk about it, maybe I wasn't gay—but she wanted to let me know it was okay to tell her if I was, to have the conversation. So, she asked me about my brother and freed me to talk to her about it. And when I told her I was gay she accepted me with open and loving arms."

In his same eulogy Ted paid tribute to his dad, my brother, who had cared for his wife in a saintly manner for over a decade through all the stages of the disease. In the last year or so his wife gibbered aloud constantly in a language that was incomprehensible. Ted ended the eulogy by saying to his father, "I finally figured out what Mom was trying to say, Dad. She was saying, 'Thank you. Thank you. Thank you. I love you. I love you. I love you.'"

The honesty of the first story, the genuine respect and love of the second anecdote, as well as the meaningful conversations, sharing of laughter and tears and genuine joy at being together in the midst of deep suffering, made me realize how important it is "to be rooted." To have a stable foundation, a strong and sturdy family tree whose branches can weather anything because of deep, deep roots.

☙

Forcing a Prayer

When I awake each day, I say a short prayer. This morning I had to force every ounce of integrity to pray it.

I am heartsick over last night's 2016 presidential election, in anguish for what this mean-spirited political view, now unchecked in all three branches of the government, will mean for the poor, for women, for refugees, for the sick, for all the vulnerable. I am frightened of what military force we will unleash around the world without an ounce of concern for the unarmed civilians in its wake. And I am fearful that what we really woke up to this morning is the unraveling of the American dream, a country sharply, irrevocably divided about what the Constitution, freedom of the press, the Statue of Liberty, and democracy itself mean.

I am appalled at the misogyny at the base of this election and angry at my church for its deafening silence over a presidential candidate who is disgusting in his treatment of women. But then, my church is misogynistic too, and yes, disgusting in its treatment of women. No women priests, ever! Really? Just the latest in an abiding history of church sexism. But how do you explain the silence of my church when a candidate condones torture, preemptive first strikes, banning of refugees, building of walls, repealing of healthcare—all contrary to church teachings? Ah, the candidate is "pro-life." What does that even mean?

I am bewildered by my own lack of perception. Who are these people who voted for Trump? Who are these neighbors, board members, co-workers, people that I celebrate weekly liturgy with at the monastery, that I thought I knew? And even liked and considered friends? How did I not know what they really believed and valued? My relationship with them is forever altered, and it breaks my heart. So, it was in deep agony, almost disbelief, that Old Monk forced herself to pray:

> This is the day our God has made.
> Let us rejoice and be glad. (Ps 118:24)

God Trusting Us

Lots of people commented on Old Monk's journal entry that followed the national election. I've read all of them, and they evoked some responses.

First, Old Monk wants to thank all of you who wrote a comment. It's a small act of courage to own what you think and feel and say it to others. Because I believe we are in for a hazardous four years, I, too, want to be honest about what I think a monastic stance requires in perilous times.

Many of you suggested praying for the situation and trusting in God. Prayer—yes, of course. I've devoted a lot of years to prayer. In formal prayer alone, I've been present to over ten-thousand prayer sessions in my fifty-five years as a Benedictine sister. And that doesn't count all the private meditation, chanting, rosaries, and mantras. And so what? For me, there is only one measure for authentic prayer: am I becoming kinder, more tolerant, more courageous, more godlike? I pray to change myself, and you can see that's taking quite a long time. I do not pray to change other people, life's circumstances, world events, or the future.

As I get older, I have a private measuring stick for my own spiritual integrity—do I speak my truth without fear and act on what I believe? That's all I pray for these days. Of course, I'd like to do it with all the kindness I can muster, but my bottom line is speaking truth to power. It's the one irrevocable lesson I've learned from getting to know Jesus of Nazareth over the years.

Too many people make Jesus of Nazareth, God's image on earth, a sentimental guru who went around being nice to everyone, saying only sweet things—a real people-pleaser. When, in reality, religious and political leaders murdered Jesus for confronting those in power, for not accepting the status quo, for breaking their unjust laws, for riling up the people, for giving hope to the poor and vulnerable. They drove huge nails into his hands and feet and sliced him open with a sword because he acted on God's word. "The Spirit of God is upon me," Jesus announced, "because God has anointed me to preach good news to the poor. God has sent me to proclaim deliverance to captives and recovery of sight to the blind, to release the oppressed" (Lk 4:18).

As for trusting in God, I think it's the reverse. I believe God is trusting in us. God is trusting that in giving us the gift of life, we will bear good fruit. That we who claim to be on a spiritual path will accept our responsibility to co-create the kind of world that God envisioned. It's up to us, each one of us, to be faithful to God's trust and do everything in our power to bring in the day when "justice and mercy embrace." "The purpose of prayer," Saint Teresa of Avila told her sisters, "is good works, good works, good works." And I believe her.

For those who feel it's too early to judge the president-elect, I offer one of my favorite lines in scripture—"Jesus did not trust himself to them because he knew what was in their heart" (Jn 2:24). Sorry, but I'm very cautious and wary of the people now taking over every branch of our government. Showing respect to them, not trying to maim or kill them with words or weapons, is enough for me. I'm not going to pretend that I trust them. I don't. Does that mean I have closed my heart to them? No, that's why I keep praying to keep my heart softer and more flexible. But I won't trust myself to them until by their actions I see a new reality. What I've witnessed over the past months—attacks on people who differ, a corruption of decency and respect, threats to immigrants and minorities, diminishment of women, dangerous warmongering—are unacceptable to me and I will resist that agenda. All of this must change before I step toward trust.

And as for healing and reconciliation, that's a process, isn't it? The South African reconciliation program took years. And it took honesty and humility. Those who committed crimes during apartheid had to acknowledge publicly their sins, crime, and errors, ask forgiveness, and make a firm purpose of amendment. I will not settle for cheap reconciliation.

Meanwhile, I drove to the Cleveland Museum of Art on the weekend and placed myself in the midst of beauty. I stood in awe at the arrival of the supermoon, its first visit in sixty-nine years. I went to the local university to hear Doris Kearns Goodwin give a historical overview of the presidency. I signed up to attend the Women's March on Washington on January 21, 2017. In other words, I continue to choose life. I bow and bend my knee in gratitude, ever mindful of God's overwhelming blessings.

CR

Easter Shouts Live

Just when I'd about given up on Easter Sunday and bodily resurrections I read about tardigrades, more commonly known as water bears. The *National Geographic* website calls them earth's "most tenacious creatures." And BBC titled its story about them "Tardigrades Return from the Dead." Believe me, that headline got my immediate attention. The story points out that if we went into space unprotected, we'd die as our blood would bubble and boil. And if by some miracle we survived that gruesome end, ionizing radiation would rip apart the DNA in our cells. So, imagine the scientists' surprise when they strapped thousands of the 1mm-long water bears to a rocket and many not only survived but the females among them laid eggs that bore healthy "baby" tardigrades. It seems these living creatures can withstand ocean depth, below freezing temperatures and radiation. They can also live without water. And they've been around for 500 million years. You can't kill them, hardly.

And if they do die or are killed, that's not the end of the story. Deprived of water the tardigrades dry up and turn dormant and glass-like. Apparently they can remain in this "dead" state for years. How do we know this? Because in 1995 water bears that were dead for eight years were brought back to life by a scientist.

The doubting Thomas in me has new information to ponder. If water bears turned to glass can rise from the dead, why not particles of dust?

Be that what it may, Old Monk will still concentrate her life on what she believes about the resurrection story. And it's this: Easter grabs us by the throat and shouts, "Live." The radiant Jesus who leaves the tomb challenges our complacency with the forces of death, be they hopelessness, fear, discouragement, or lack of will. Don't let death have the last word in your story, Jesus urges. None of us has the right to sleep in death. Even if there is no angel to help you, grab the door of the tomb that holds you back and rip its seal. There's too much goodness in you that still needs to rise, and there's too much work in the world that still needs to be done.

CR

Overwhelmed

When I'm feeling overwhelmed or sorry for myself for "having too much to do," I read this prayer by Saint Teresa of Avila.

How is it, my God, that you have given me this hectic life and so little time to enjoy your presence. All day, people are waiting to speak to me, and even during meals I have to keep talking to people about their concerns and needs. During sleep itself I am still thinking and dreaming about the problems that wait for me tomorrow. I am doing all this for you, not for myself.

My way of life is more tormenting than rewarding, and I only hope that for you it is a gift of love. I know you are always beside me, yet I become so busy that I forget you and ignore you. If you want me to keep up this pace, please make me think about you and love you, even during the most hectic activity. If you do not want me to be so busy, please release me from it and teach me how others can take over some of my responsibilities.

Lots of delicate lines in this prayer. Especially the one that reads, "I am doing all this for you, not for myself." That's always a cliffhanger for me. How do I really know the motivation for keeping busy, no matter what I say? Do I still turn the office key because I have a healthy sense of responsibility to bring the reign of God on earth as it is in heaven, or do I fear facing a vast emptiness, a loss of identity and meaning, if I relinquish the office key?

And I wonder, too, about her last sentence: "If you do not want me to be so busy, please release me from it and teach me how others can take over some of my responsibilities." What is Teresa praying for here? Is she praying that God gives her an illness or that she dies, because really the only one that can cut back on busyness is Teresa herself. Or is she just asking God to teach her how to delegate? Really! That does not seem to be a prayer petition worthy of a doctor of the church.

No, "being so busy" is not God's problem. This dilemma is Teresa's alone. And I think she knows that. But it's good therapy to rant against God rather than complain to other people. With people, you're liable to get maudlin sympathy, bad advice, or a plan of escape. With God, your words are met with the Great Silence and thrown back on you. As is fitting. And, of course, God stays present no matter your choice. That's God's role.

Meanwhile it's a holiday weekend and Old Monk is locking Saint Teresa's prayer in the file cabinet and promising herself to be mindful of God's presence on the golf course.

☙

What Happens to Your Heart

I have always loved stories more than facts. For example, all that I remember from my high school physics class is Archimedes sitting in a bathtub and suddenly shouting, "Eureka—I have found it." Then he jumped out of the tub and ran through the streets naked, proclaiming, "I've got it—Eureka." I really can't explain what he discovered. Something about the fact that you can calculate the volume of an object by determining how much water it displaces. I do know it was an important discovery, but I loved the story the most. I got a glimpse into what creative genius looked like in the flesh as well as unbridled joy in discovery.

That's why I was so happy to find this quote by Barbara Brown Taylor in a reflection she wrote on whether the Epiphany story is "true." She writes:

> It's not that the facts don't matter. It is just that they don't matter as much as the stories do, and stories can be true whether they happen or not. You do not have to do archeology to find out if they are genuine or spend years in the library combing ancient texts. . . . You just listen to the story. You let it come to life inside of you, and then you decide on the basis of your own tears or laughter whether the story is true. If you are in any doubt, it is always a good idea to watch other people who have listened to the story—just pay attention to how the story affects them over time. Does it make them more or less human? Does it open them up or shut them down? Does it increase their capacity for joy?

I'm thinking about stories today because July 11 is the feast of Saint Benedict. What usually comes to mind when you mention Benedict of Nursia is the Rule he wrote on how to build an alternative society by living in community and devoting yourself to prayer, holy leisure, and good works. The Rule has guided Western monasticism for over fifteen hundred years, and its worldwide impact is monumental. Most monastic communities, including mine, read it aloud every day in small sections. Over the course of the year, we hear the Rule three times in its entirety. But truth be told, I find it kind of boring.

Old Monk prefers the stories of Benedict's life in the *Dialogues of Gregory*, which were put together by Saint Gregory the Great, a Benedictine who became a pope. I love these metaphorical tales and wish we'd read them aloud and play with them in kind of a midrash fashion. Why is it a miracle that Benedict repaired a broken tray for his nurse? Are miracles really that ordinary, and is each of us capable of performing these daily acts of kindness? There are stories about how to respond when evil is done to you; about breaking rules for a greater good; about discipleship and friendship; about the preferential option for the poor, especially in times of scarcity; about reaching out to the enemy; about seeing the entire world in a single ray of light. Each of these stories takes a lifetime to mine. But we hardly touch them—embarrassed, I think, by their simple and fanciful presentation. And we're the poorer for it.

See, it's one thing to write a Rule on holiness. It's another thing to live a good life. Did Benedict live a good life? And how do we know if he did? And what does it mean to me and thee? Let me tell you a story . . . and see what happens to your heart.

℣

The Golden Arches

I love theater, and I've been fortunate to see a few plays in New York, Toronto, Niagara on the Lake, London, Chautauqua Institution, and at our own Erie Playhouse, of course. A couple of these plays were award winning, and a handful were labeled classics.

But do you know which play Old Monk holds most dear? The play was performed in an experimental theater in a deteriorating building in a bad section of Erie. I have no idea who wrote it or what it was called. All I remember is that one of the characters was a homeless old woman. And in the scene that is forever burned in my heart, she is talking about the Golden Arches of McDonald's. Yes, McDonald's.

In the play this haggard old woman is waxing eloquent on how the lit Golden Arches—in the midst of lonely nights and dangerous streets—resemble a mystical vision for street walkers. The light speaks to her of presence and care and comfort and compassion and safety—all of which she equates with the Divine. Yes, McDonald's equals a glimpse of the Divine!!

She talks about how the hamburger haven takes you in, no questions asked, and allows you to stay so long as you sip a cup of coffee and don't cause trouble. She contrasts it to all the churches that line the streets in town. All the churches are dark and the doors locked, she explains. Only McDonald's is bathed in welcoming light.

I saw that play over twenty years ago and go back to that scene over and over again, especially when someone badmouths McDonald's. And someone did this week in my presence, so I retold the story.

I'm thinking that it affected me the way Jesus's parables and actions must have affected his audiences. To Old Monk's ears, McDonald's is a contemporary Samaritan, a woman taken in adultery, an unclean tax collector. The story shocks—awakens—just like Jesus's stories blew the minds of those accustomed to badmouthing the "unclean," the "evil ones," the "sinners" that we regard with self-righteous contempt. McDonald's is a lot holier than a church, folks, go figure, and do likewise.

ॐ

Exegesis of Eating

This winter I subscribed to an excellent literary journal, *Poetry East*, and the first issue that arrived in the mail was devoted to food. Poems on food. Great art on food. Quotes on food. I read it slowly every morning, savoring every mouthful.

The magazine reminded me of an essay on food that I read years ago and never forgot, though I frequently berated myself for not saving it or at least copying a few passages. Then two months ago I started to organize my old journals and found that I had copied one quote from the article, "The Exegesis of Eating," by Alane Salierno

Mason, which appeared in the book *Best Spiritual Writing 2001*. She wrote: "To prepare, for one's elders, the kind of food they prepared for you in the way they taught you to prepare it is something that goes beyond food for survival. It is the richer nourishment of memory, love, and gratitude."

Here was someone who articulated what Old Monk feels about food and can't communicate to people who did not grow up in an ethnic family where food was the axis on which our world turned. Mason captured the spiritual nature of food by wrapping it in the words "memory, love, and gratitude." Those three words explain why I am reduced to tears when I talk about my mother's chicken and biscuits or potato pancakes or elderberry pies or pierogi or . . . How it was for me to wake up every morning and smell bacon and eggs, or French toast, or biscuits coming from the kitchen—no cold cereal for me or my brothers. How it was coming home every day from school and being greeted by a homemade cake, or oatmeal raisin cookies, or some exotic pastries filled with creams and jams. And this love for food extended to grandparents and aunts and uncles and picnics and parties and holiday feasts. Always overladen tables.

Here's how I spent the week between Christmas and New Year's when I was a child: Keeping the Polish tradition of *Kolendy* (carols), the entire clan of Kownackis or Kryzans (my mother's family) gathered each night after work at the home of one of our relatives. We entered the house singing Polish carols and were treated to a delicious buffet of sausages and hams and turkey and casseroles and homemade breads and sweets. After everyone ate, we sang more Polish carols and then . . . we went to another relative's home and repeated the entire process. Sometimes we visited three homes a night, eating and drinking and singing and eating. We did this for seven straight nights—Christmas Day to New Year's Eve—culminating with a New Year's party at my home where my mother prepared the most amazing shrimp crepes. You can understand why it's really hard for me to get excited over kale smoothies and energy bars and fat-free anything. Because for me, though it's about delicious hot food prepared with tender care, it's mainly about a gift I received wrapped in memory, love, and gratitude.

CR

Gross Compassion Product

In an interview Wendell Berry wonders why we don't have a "gross earth product" that counts, for example, the number of trees and the apples, since our lives depend on things of the earth. Why celebrate a rising gross national product when we should be mourning a declining gross earth product? He notes that we wring our hands over a trade deficit, yet it pales when compared to the earth deficit. Berry's words make Old Monk wonder why we don't have a gross kindness product or a gross compassion product that counts our random acts of goodness and measures our spiritual development as a people.

Elizabeth Lesser said that the quest for spirituality is an instinct like eating or sleeping. She said religions were formed to respond to the instinct, to know that life has meaning, to know that everything is connected, to fill us with childlike wonder at the gift of life. And Old Monk nodded her head in total agreement. Then she read a letter to the editor in the morning paper and wonders how it all goes wrong. The letter writer describes herself as a true Christian whose prayers were answered when Trump was elected because he will get rid of all immigrants, LGBTQ degenerates, people who don't stand during the national anthem, abortion, and nations that are godless. He is likened to the second coming.

Now about this instinct. Lesser, let's talk.

CR

Let's Keep Listening

The body of a woman who used to come with her two children to our soup kitchen washed up on the lakeshore this month. She suffered severe mental illness and committed suicide. This was the first tragic death at the kitchen for two new staff members. They took it very hard, shedding deep tears and struggling with the perennial question, "Could we have done more to prevent this?"

Sister Mary Miller, who has given thirty-five years to the soup kitchen, said, "I have seen so much tragedy at the kitchen, but I never want to become jaded to the pain of losing a guest, a friend that we all know and care about." She then talked about the brutal murder of a young woman she was close to, the numerous suicides of guests, the abuse she has witnessed, the horrific struggles with addictions that never end. "I was grateful to see the tears of the new people on staff," she said, "because what we weep for tells us what we care about."

Indeed, Old Monk thought. If you listen carefully enough you can hear wails of pain in soup kitchens across the land—endless weeping from the homeless, the sick, the hungry, and, of course, the ocean of loneliness that engulfs so many. And our tears must mingle with theirs if we have any chance of becoming more human, of fashioning hearts compassionate and empathetic enough to create the world that Christmas carols envision.

So, weeping and wailing should engulf the land. Can you imagine the White House and halls of Congress awash with tears because of the suffering their callous actions cause to the poor and vulnerable? This would be the one sure sign that Christmas in the United States is bigger and better than ever. Let's listen. Do you hear what I hear? Applause, laughter, rejoicing because the rich are given more silver and gold while a child, so many children, shiver in the cold. But Old Monk also listens to another authority. She listens to the word of promise proclaimed so clearly by the prophet Isaiah in this holy season. And this is what she hears and holds fast to:

> Woe to you who pass unjust policies
> and draft oppressive legislation,
> who withhold justice from the powerless

and rob poor people—my people—of their
    rights,
you who take advantage of widows
and steal from orphans.
What will you do on Judgment Day,
when disaster comes upon you from afar?
Who do you expect will help you?
Where will you hide your wealth?

....

Then the stump of Jesse will yield a shoot;
from the roots of Jesse, a branch will blossom.
God's spirit will rest upon you—
so that the poor people are treated with fairness
and the downtrodden have their rights upheld.
A single word will strike down tyrants;
and wickedness will disappear.
Justice will be the belt around your waist—
faithfulness will gird you. . . .

There will be no harm, no destruction
anywhere on my holy mountain;
for as the water fills the sea,
so the land will be filled with knowledge of
    God. (Isa 10:1–3; 11:1–5, 9)

Let's keep listening. . . .

☙

Imitation and Repetition

One of the best couple hours I spend each month is with my women's writing circle. It's an open circle, so the number of participants varies. This month thirteen women walked in, and at least six were first timers. What draws them is an itch to write, of course, but being in the company of other women can't be underestimated. "I like it that this is just for women," said one of the newcomers. "Although we're each different, we have so much in common that we share."

I was heartened by her comment because I do strive to make the circle a safe place where anything you write counts. It counts for the writer, first, and sometimes there's a bonus where what you write touches someone else's heart.

Mostly, I look at the circle as a practice session where women can explore their experiences and try to find their voice through the written word. We read some good writing by poets mostly, and then we imitate. And then we practice again. It's more like a spiritual practice, another way of getting to know the beauty inside.

My approach to writing was blessed in an article I read by Jim Sollisch, "Piano Lessons: Do Writers Need a Teacher or a Coach?" that appeared in the March/April issue of *Poetry and Writers* magazine. I was hooked the minute I read, "When I taught writing, I told my students there was no reason to worry about punctuation until they had written something worth punctuating correctly."

I knew immediately that I had a soul brother, because Sollisch tapped into my experience. When I was a sister in training, all the postulants, novices, and scholastics were taking a literature course for college credit. One of our assignments was a writing exercise that grabbed my creative juices in a most bizarre way. I knew it was pushing the envelope—this is not the proper subject or way for sisters to write—and I couldn't wait to see how the teacher would react. I aimed to shock. Imagine my surprise when she shocked me. "This is a fine piece of writing," she said, "and you might have a bit of talent, but you get an F- for grammar and punctuation. If you want people to understand what you write, go and learn the grammar rules you should have mastered in fourth grade." The sister was my director, and she taught me a lesson of a lifetime. That summer I enrolled in a basic prerequisite grammar class for college newbies and in six weeks knew enough grammar and punctuation to let me get by in semiliterate fashion.

It's Sollisch's belief, and mine too, that we should approach writing classes more like coaches than teachers, more practice than theory, more doing than thinking. He compares it to acquiring the skill of basketball, and I resonate. To play basketball, he says, "you need only to watch others play and to practice. Imitation and repetition." That's how I learned all sports. So, my two greatest loves—sports and writing—required coaches, not teachers. This, as Sollisch points out, is not true for the study of physics or other sciences where theory first is essential. But writing, piano playing, shooting hoops, are skills that can be practiced and then overlapped with some theory.

Anyway, all of this got me thinking about Jesus. Was he more teacher or coach? I'm going to lay odds on coach. Here's why. When asked about how to live a good life, he said, "Love God and love your neighbor as yourself." That magic little word *love* takes it out of thinking and into doing, out of the concept trap and into the physical world. I don't know about you, but I'm still practicing how to love. Lots of trials and errors over seventy-six years. But I'm still trying to imitate those whom I think are true lovers—people like Robert Lax and Dorothy Day and Mary Oliver—and I keep practicing just like my coach Jesus encourages.

CB

Name of God, Likeness of God

A book I'm reading by Rabbi Rami Shapiro gave me a good insight into the Palm Sunday procession where the crowds waved tree branches and shouted to Jesus, "Blessed is the one who comes in the name of God."

In his book *The Sacred Art of Lovingkindness*, Shapiro tells us that the Book of Genesis teaches that we are made in the image and likeness of God. But in the Torah, when God actually creates us, it refers to us only as the image of God, not the likeness. What's the difference? Being the image of God, Shapiro writes, means that we are God manifest. We are the living God in time—that's what it means to be made in the image of God. You, me—you and me—we are the image of God in our time.

By now you might be asking: "If this is true, why isn't the world perfect? If we are all the name of God, the image of God, why the injustice, the cruelty, the torture, the meanness, the violence toward each other?"

Because it's only half the scripture, isn't it? Being the name of God, being made in the image of God, is a gift we've all been given. But the other half of the scripture—that we are also made in the *likeness* of God—is a choice.

Shapiro writes, "Being the likeness of God means that we have the potential to act in a godly manner."

In other words, it's up to us if we want to become the likeness of God. Which brings me back to Jesus in the Palm Sunday scripture. The people already recognize in him the image of God. "Blessed is the one who comes in the name of God," they shout as they wave palm branches.

But how about the likeness of God? Did Jesus become the likeness of God? Did he show us what it means to act in a godly manner? I watched Jesus carefully this Lent. And here's what Jesus of Nazareth told me about acting godly.

That the purpose of life is to figure out this koan, "Love one another as I have loved you." That's a godly task.

That people you trust will betray you, but you keep trusting. That's acting godly.

That anger at injustice is a holy act. But you don't stand up to the temple capitalists and power-hungry religious and state authorities without paying a price. But it's in the likeness of God.

That carrying your cross in public—all your suffering exposed to the mocking crowd—is nothing to be ashamed of. It's what God does.

That sharing a meal with friends can sustain you through anything. How godly!

That it's good to waste money on perfume and other things of beauty and pleasure. That is what God says.

That telling stories is the best way to imitate God. That is the likeness of God.

That you should spend more time with sinners and tax collectors and prostitutes and those on the edge of society than with keepers of the temple. Look at God.

That you should hold both cheering and jeering crowds with a loose hand. God did.

That if you want to understand what the reign of God is like, you must close your ears to the compromising and weary words of adults who have sold their souls and suffer the children to come unto you with fresh vision. And you must listen to them. God insists.

That you never refuse a well-meaning act of kindness, like a cloth being wiped across your worn face—even if it seems useless. Especially if it seems useless.

That your last act on earth—they know not what they do—should be unconditional forgiveness.

That human touch and healing, not suffering, are what save us.

That the tears and words of women and their daughters are of special concern.

That if you get a chance at new life, a new beginning, come back as a gardener, one who plants possibility and tends it. That is what God did.

These are some of the ways I saw Jesus acting in the likeness of God. I'm sure you have others. What I do believe is that at the end, Jesus knew himself to be both the image and likeness of God.

His words to Mary Magdalene when she came to the tomb on the third day are telling. Jesus says to Magdalene, "It is I."

These are the words of a person who has searched hard and deep, who has faced his own darkness in the deserts of life, who has loved and suffered and loved again; who has lived a full life of friendship and enemy wrestling, who embraces endless mercy, who has seen his heart expand to the point where it is impossible not to cry out on behalf of the powerless and who has paid the price for the great compassion, and who, in the end, lets it all flow into the hands of God—into your hands I commend myself.

"It is I." Blessed is the one who comes in the name of God. Blessed is the one who comes in the likeness of God.

CR

Poets in the Morning

Old Monk enjoys a brief conversation most mornings with poets, hermits, and Zen types, and seekers of all stripes. Here are some recent ones:

When despair for the world grows, Wendell Berry writes, "I come into the peace of wild things. . . . I come into the presence of still water. . . . For a time I rest in the grace of the world, am free." Lucky you, Wendell. When my despair for the world grows, when I get fed up with the headlines, I rant to anyone in earshot or pour a glass of potato vodka. Now and then I go into the presence of the divine Mother and pray my beads for mercy.

I wish I could join eighth-century Chinese poet Li Po, who made his home in the mountain forest. He called it "the other world." Truth is, Li Po, that's why I joined the monastery. I too left one world to seek another where "The peach trees blossom. The water flows." Like you I wanted nothing except a quiet, untethered soul. I've been here almost sixty years, and every spring I think that I smell a peach blossom, though I've never seen one. And one afternoon in late October, about ten years ago, I followed the sound of running water. . . . Oh, Li Po, did you write a poem about where you lived or where you desired to dwell?

I'm wild about the Zen master Suzuki, who summarized, as I mentioned before, "the secret of Zen in just two words: not always so."

How we want certainty, right answers, the truth. When in reality there is no truth that is definite for all time. We fall in love and think it will last forever. . . . Not always so. We're taught and believe the one path to holiness is the desert and find ourselves in an exotic brothel. . . . Not always so. We map out our careers and end up in a strange neighborhood. . . . Not always so. We hold tightly an indisputable teaching about the nature of God, and it turns to ashes. . . . Not always so. I read once that it's how we react to the "not always so" moments that determine our lives. We have that brief second of time when we are confronted with a "not always so"—either our world splits or gently shifts—and we resist, or we turn. Either way, we are different.

Eaten Alive

"Don't start working with the poor unless you're willing to be eaten alive." A sister who had spent long years bandaging wounds and trying to jump-start seemingly hopeless lives gave me that advice over forty years ago, and I've never forgotten it. Though I'm still not sure I understand it completely. I think she meant that if you steer your life toward those in the margins and hold back or don't engage with an expanded heart, it won't work. If you don't feel up to the call to be present to whatever is needed, whenever it is needed, don't open a soup kitchen. Because that will mean phone calls in the middle of the night or delaying an evening out to find a shelter for someone being evicted or sleepless nights worrying about children who tell you frightening stories while you feed them peanut butter and jelly sandwiches. It is not a nine-to-five workday. You have to give without measure. And you have to give with love. That's the most important thing because the poor, better than most, can spot when you're doing it out of duty, not love.

Saint Vincent de Paul understood it:

You will find out that charity is a heavy burden to carry, heavier than the kettle of soup and the full basket. But you will keep your gentleness and your smile. It is not enough to give soup and bread. This the rich can do. You are the servant of the poor, always smiling and good-humored. They are your masters, terribly sensitive and exacting masters you will see. And the uglier and the dirtier they will be, the more unjust and insulting, the more love you must give them. It is only for your love alone that the poor will forgive you the bread you give to them.

Anyway, I don't think I have what it takes, and I learned that pretty early on. What I decided to do is be eaten alive by one person. And I made that commitment to a young boy thirty-two years ago and still feel love is my motivation. But I do admire those whose hearts are wide enough to embrace the world's or the city's or the neighborhood's sufferings. We call them saints or bodhisattvas, the pure of heart, whose egos, self-importance, agendas have been "eaten alive" until only a terrifying love remains.

☙

Find Out Who You Are

"Winter is the best time / To find out who you are," wrote the poet David Budbill, making a profound bow toward quiet, and silence, and contemplation as essential tools to enlightenment. But I sit looking out my study window in mid-spring where everything is in riot—the trees, the gardens, the wind, the birds, the clouds, the rain, the pouring sun, the front yards, the children, especially the children. For Old Monk greater self-discovery happens when a spray of water from the neighbor's hose suddenly skips across my flowering pear tree and awakens the black bee hiding there, safely wrapped in solitude.

☙

Inner Argument

I left the house today in plenty of time to arrive at the Silent Peace Walk, a monthly event organized by our local Benedictines for Peace group. For almost a year now, people have gathered at a designated place in Erie—a neighborhood, a park, a landmark—and walked in silence for twenty minutes. The purpose is to reflect on the violence lurking in our hearts and hopefully take a step or two toward becoming a more authentic peacemaker. I drove toward Perry Square, the gathering center of downtown Erie, and was met by barricaded streets and no-parking signs everywhere.

Of course, I said to myself, the city is prepared for Roar on the Shore, which begins tomorrow when ten-thousand motorcycles rumble into Erie. Then I started an inner fight with my friend Sister Anne, who organized the walk.

"What's the matter with you, Anne? Why would you hold a walk here when there's no parking and everything's blocked off?"

And on and on it went in my head, with a few swear words thrown in. I finally found somewhere to park the car and walked to Perry Square. No one was there. "What the . . . ?"

Then it dawned on me. The Silent Peace Walk was at the Perry Monument, not Perry Square. The monument is on our beautiful

Lake Erie peninsula, about thirty minutes away. I missed it. Except I didn't—this was an excellent Silent Peace Walk for me. It took about twenty minutes to get there and be blasted with an unpleasant "Aha! moment." Here I am going to a Silent Peace Walk in the hope of becoming a better peacemaker and all the while I'm engaged in an inner argument and tossing insults at my friend, Anne.

"While you are proclaiming peace with your lips, be sure to have it more fully in your heart," Francis of Assisi tells us. And Thomas Merton reminds, "Instead of hating all the people you think are warmongers, hate the appetites and disorders in your own soul which are the causes of war." No doubt about it, Old Monk needs a silent peace walk more than most. Next month she can try again.

◌

Stand There

Dan Berrigan recounts this:

> "Don't just do something," the Buddha said,
> "stand there."

A friend gave me this saying on a paperweight in the 1970s and I've kept it nearby ever since. Berrigan gave the quote after participating in the Catonsville Nine action when he and eight others took draft records from a government office and burned them with napalm to protest the Vietnam War. He said it to explain why he participated in the action in broad daylight and stood there until police officers arrived to arrest them.

I thought of this quote a lot after a visit from an old friend, the artist Sister Helen David Brancato, IHM. I first met Helen when we traveled to Haiti in 1989 as part of a Pax Christi USA delegation to document human-rights abuses. Haiti was under military rule then, and the poor were gathering around a charismatic priest, Jean-Bertrand Aristide, and preparing to bring in a new Haiti. In other words, there was a lot of unrest, a lot of threats, arrests, and killings of suspected revolutionaries and followers of Aristide.

On one of our visits we entered the stronghold of resistance and met with peasants to hear their stories. It was a dangerous trip for the obvious reasons but also perilous because of the conditions of the so-called roads that we had to travel during the dark in a van that was breathing its last. We made it through the night but continued to share stories of sleeping with tarantulas and Tonton Macoute drumbeats substituting for a lullaby.

On the way back to Port-au-Prince, however, the van broke down in a seaside village. That meant a long, long wait because there was no AAA or gas station anywhere near. A couple village guys came out to help and dozens of children and teenagers appeared, curious about these white strangers. We couldn't speak Creole, so what to do? What I remember is Helen David taking out her sketch pad and drawing pencil portraits of each of the children. It was instant communication. Most of these children had never seen their own images. They didn't have mirrors in their huts, let alone cameras. I remember their smiles and cries of delight as they shared their pictures with one another. So, when I think of the quote, "Don't just do something, stand there," I think of Helen standing on the Haitian seashore, drawing pencil in hand.

Actually, I think it's the quote that best describes her life. Helen David has always "stood there" for the poor and marginalized. All her art forces us to see their suffering and grapple with the grave injustices that cripple their hopes and dreams. A number of years ago she opened a drop-in art center in a poor Philadelphia neighborhood, and it was there that she met an illiterate woman named Ida who turned out to be a talented artist. "She was a savant," Helen

David said, "an urban shaman with raw talent and a free spirit." Helen David promoted Ida's work with a passion, organizing solo exhibits at art galleries and museums, getting wealthy individuals to sponsor Ida's work. Ida died a few years ago, but Helen David is still standing there. She brought me a hand-printed and illustrated book that she wrote on Ida, a kind of memoir of Ida's art and their friendship.

In our troubled times we often search for answers to the question, "What can I do to change things?" I'm not sure there is any better advice than that given by the Buddha, "Don't just do something, stand there." Make sure you know what you stand for and just keep standing there.

CR

Inbreaking

My friend Mary leaned over to me, tears in her eyes, when the congregation was singing the soul-stirring hymn, "Holy, Holy, Holy! Lord God Almighty," and said, "We can't let them wreck what is still so beautiful." We were at the Sunday Morning Worship Service at Chautauqua Institution, and she was referring to the horrific Pennsylvania Grand Jury Report on Sexual Abuse in the Catholic Church that had just been released. What does she mean, I wondered? What is still so beautiful that we must hold on to for dear life while we rage against the crimes committed against innocent children and demand justice for the abusers and the hierarchy whose "I was only following orders" made it possible? I looked around at the beautiful faces of more than one thousand people in that huge amphitheater who were singing their hearts out to God. To God, not to any institution. Trust in the institutional church may crumble over the sexual abuse scandal, and it should. But what the sinful system cannot be permitted to destroy is the beauty of the living communion of saints. The beauty of all those people placing their trust and love and faith where it belongs, "Holy, Holy, Holy! Lord God almighty! Early in the morning our song shall rise to thee."

We went to Chautauqua to hear Rev. Winnie Varghese, senior priest for justice and reconciliation at Trinity Church Wall Street. She chose the Annunciation as the reading and urged us to listen to women's words, especially Mary's. She pointed out that on the two big feasts of the year—Christmas and Easter—when most of the Christian family gathers, the church selects readings where women's voices are heard. It is the warmth and tenderness of our God that we draw on, that we need to hear at these grand moments. Varghese is an Episcopalian and said that Mary was not a focal point of her religious formation, but now she wants to be with her, to listen to her. She cautioned about making Mary bodiless, a deity, or "blessed," or "virgin." She recounted how as a response to the #MeToo movement, she began to address Mary as simply "the woman, Mary." "It helped people recall their own stories of powerlessness and abuse. Some people responded with tears and some not," she said. "Some got angry because we called Mary only a woman."

She told an inspiring story about a Mary celebration in her native country of India. It takes place on the feast of the Nativity of Mary, September 8, and coincides with a celebration of a goddess in the neighboring Hindu temple. "The women say Mary and the goddess are sisters," Varghese said. The priests will have none of it. Ten thousand women come to the festival and take over the area. These are poor women, oppressed women, who for a few days create a new reality.

"The order of the world is turned upside down," she said. "That festival becomes a vision of the reign of God." Then, Varghese continued, "The world goes back to normal and patriarchy rules. I want to stand in that upside-down moment," she concluded. "That is the inbreaking. It is a moment when we see truth so great that the soul cries out."

I wept through the homily. It gave me a sense of peace and renewal and hope. Oh, how the church suffers because it refuses to allow an inbreaking of the leadership and wisdom of women.

In the car ride home Mary said to me, "About thirty years ago I heard Sister Mary Luke Tobin speak at a conference of religious teachers. She told us, 'The church will be brought to its knees by women and children.' I didn't understand what she meant, but I never forgot it. Now I know."

Following the worship service, we went to the coffee shop and met a woman we knew. She went right to the church's sexual abuse scandal and asked us, "Where can I go? Should I stay in the church? So many priests named in the report were my friends. One of them married my husband and me." It's a question that many are wrestling with. It's a question I ask myself daily. And it comes back to that beautiful communion of saints. When Dan Berrigan was asked why he stayed in the Jesuits, he replied, "It was the friendship, community, the promise of support for one another, a vision of great work to be done, which those before you had done so well." For me, that suffices.

છ

Peace Hero

I just finished reading *At Play in the Lion's Den: A Biography and Memoir of Daniel Berrigan* by Jim Forest, and I'm surprised at the chapter in the book that I keep thinking about. Dan is my peace hero. I got involved in protests and civil disobedience, starting in the late 1960s, due in large part to his prophetic witness.

I was expecting to get fired up again reading about his dramatic actions and poetic proclamations of draft-card burnings, going underground rather than report to prison, literally beating swords into plowshares. But no. The chapter I liked best was "Listener of

Last Resort," and it detailed his hospice work with cancer patients and AIDS sufferers.

For four years Dan was a regular presence at St. Rose's Home, a hospice for patients dying of cancer. Founded in 1896 by Rose Hawthorne Lathrop, the daughter of famed American novelist Nathaniel Hawthorne, the hospice cares for the working poor and penniless. The nursing care is all free; and no money is collected from insurance companies or from city, state, or federal coffers. You'd expect a cleric to visit the dying to hear confessions or anoint. But Dan didn't go as "Father." He listened to the guests, held their hands, shared silence, made beds, cleaned, prayed, and comforted the relatives of the dying.

In the early 1980s, when the AIDS epidemic hit, Dan shifted his presence to St. Vincent Hospital, the hospice for most of New York's AIDS victims. For twelve years he went weekly to walk the wards with the patients, listen to their stories, always keeping a special eye out for those who had no visitors. He visited AIDS patients at home, cooked meals for them and their loved ones in his apartment, took them shopping and to restaurants, and buried many of them. A friend recalls, "As the men grew sicker, he fed and bathed them. He washed their soiled clothes. He sat with them for hours in the hospital as they declined. The suffering that comes upon his friends is horrific. Some became covered in lesions. Some went blind. Some are rendered unable to eat or suffered from endless diarrhea."

Reading this chapter turned all his arrests and prophecies into pure gold. I reread my favorite Dan Berrigan passage with new eyes: "Sometime in your life, hope that you might see one starving man, the look on his face when the bread finally arrives. Hope that you might have baked it or bought or even kneaded it yourself. For that look on his face, for your meeting his eyes across a piece of bread, you might be willing to lose a lot, or suffer a lot, or die a little, even."

Dan sat at the table with many starved men and women—the cancer victims at St. Rose's and those dying of cancer from the bombing of Hiroshima, the napalmed children with peeling skin in Vietnam, and the ulcerous skin of AIDS victims. He looked at each of them and all victims of war and poverty and endless suffering with great love; and he offered them the "bread" of his life. That meant he lost and suffered a lot, and even died a little—such a beautiful legacy.

I have a friend who tells me that she stays in the church not because of the words of the Creed. She stays in the church because of the lives of its saints. Me, too. And Dan Berrigan is one of them.

☙

Lay Waste the Day

This summer I read *The Art of the Wasted Day* by Patricia Hampl and remember two great passages. In the first chapter Hampl recalls being prepared for her First Confession and learning as an eight-year-old that daydreaming was considered an "occasion of sin." Hampl writes, "I don't hesitate. I throw my lot with the occasion of sin. I couldn't care less what it's called. It's pure pleasure. Infinite delight. For this a person goes to hell. Okay then."

Later in the book she writes about asking a cloistered nun "what her way of life was based upon—love of God, the search for meaning? What was the foundation of the contemplative life? Oh, she said without a pause—leisure, it's based on leisure." Hampl continues, "She didn't say her life was about leisure, but based on it."

Truth be told I did go to the monastery at the age of seventeen because I was attracted to a life of leisure. I imagined days spent in reading and prayer and slow walks in the cloister and lots of silence and solitude. I was only in the monastery a day or two when that image was erased. We spent most of our time working and working and working. And though we didn't talk, we were always in a

group—not much solitude. It took a few years, but I finally figured out that you had to make your own time for leisure. It didn't
necessarily come by following the daily monastic schedule. That
meant working at having real conversations, praying the psalms in
a reflective manner, building in regular time for reading and writing
and daydreaming, taking time to visit museums and art galleries,
and attending an occasional play and concert. The world will do
everything it can to convince you that all of this is an "occasion of
sin," a way of getting sidetracked from all the work that must be
done to bring in the reign of God. But, like Hampl, I believe that
staring out windows for long periods of time, that imagination and
reflection and wasting hours with friends over a good meal or over
a good poem are as essential as works of mercy.

Well, I like to think that I believe it. Yet even this morning I
woke up thankful that the worst of my cold and flu bout was over,
and I could attack my "to do" list with a vengeance, making up for
the workday that I had missed. I felt a little guilty when I found
myself too fatigued and was forced to take it easy, mostly loafing
and napping. Then I remembered one of Dorothy Day's favorite
desert sayings: "Each morning I wake up with all these solutions
and joyous I lay waste the day."

☙

Snail On

A snail on a fern is the art photo for this month in the "Meditation" wall calendar that hangs in my study nook. I'm drawn
to it because it reminds of a favorite haiku by Issa that I copied in
my commonplace book about fifty years ago. The translation by
R. H. Blyth reads:

> O snail
> Climb Mount Fuji,
> But slowly, slowly!

Mount Fuji is the highest and most sacred mountain in Japan, the site of many pilgrimages and the subject of many paintings and poems. Recently I copied a different version of the poem, this time translated by Richard Jones:

> Snail, you're my hero.
> You will give all of your life
> to climb Mount Fuji.

I carry this poem in my pocket for a few reasons. Whenever I plan a big project and get impatient with the slow process, I recite it. Whenever I'm faced with an obstacle that seems insurmountable, I remember it.

Trump's visit to Erie last week is a case in point. I was one of three hundred protesters voicing my disapproval of his administration while there were twelve thousand Trump supporters whipped into a frenzy of adulation that was frightening. If a world of peace and justice is your Mount Fuji, then the Trump thing might cause the snail in you to stop the quest or even turn back. It's too big an obstacle. But three hundred protesters is a snail-like step. Just keep moving, I tell myself, one more protester at a time.

The main reason I carry the poem is why Issa wrote it, I think. I've been on a spiritual quest for over sixty years and yet . . . and yet. No doubt about it, I'm still my sinful old self. I could get discouraged, and sometimes do. But then I remember Issa's poem. All I have to do is reach in my pocket and read it. Then snail on.

☙

This I Believe

I'm reading *This I Believe*, a book of short essays from eighty famous and ordinary people who write about a core personal belief. For example, the poet Joy Harjo believes in the sun as a relative that illuminates our path on earth. Elvia Bautista believes that everyone deserves flowers on their grave. Norman Corwin believes in common courtesy. Newt Gingrich believes that the world is inherently a very dangerous place and that things that are now very good can go bad very quickly. And so on. The book is based on the NPR series of the same name that began in 1951, ended fifty years later, and was revived in 2004.

The editors encourage you to write your own "I believe . . ." essay, so Old Monk is giving it a try:

A few months ago one of "my boys" visited me. He is one of twenty neighborhood kids that I organized into a work, study, and play program when I moved in with my dad, now deceased, about fifteen years ago. At that time the block where my dad lived, the one I grew up on, was one of the worst in the city for drugs and crime and neglect. In the program the children earned money to spend at the neighborhood store for cleaning a patch of the block each day—picking up litter, sweeping, raking leaves. They also got the special dollars for reading books that I selected, doing homework and extra schoolwork. We had summer-school sessions in my garage and went on a lot of field trips together. It was two magical years of my life. Anyway, when I opened the front door, there stood J, now in his early twenties. He gave me a big hug and said, "I was just passing by, Sister Kownacki, and wanted to see if you still lived here and say 'hi.'"

He also wanted to thank me for "saving his life." He said, "I have two children now, Sister Kownacki, and I want to be a good father." "That's wonderful, J," I said. "What are you doing with yourself?" "I ain't gonna lie to you, Sister Kownacki. I'm into drugs." I didn't know how to react. Should I express anger, disapproval, call the cops? But this was my dear J and he had come to visit. So, all I said was, "Are you satisfied with that choice, J?" He said he wasn't happy with himself but felt trapped because he had a prison record and no high school diploma.

We talked a bit about his brothers and sisters—one painful story after another—and eventually I sputtered some words about trying to get out of the drug business for the sake of his children. He promised he was going to try, but I don't have much hope. What got me, though, was that he kept telling me how I saved his life and he'd be eternally grateful. Given his tragic life story so far, I couldn't figure out what I had done for him that was so important. It sounded like I was a complete failure. So, I finally asked him, "Why do you say I saved your life, J? What did I do?" He looked at me wistfully and said, "You cared. It's so rare, Sister Kownacki, that someone care about you, really care about you, for no reason at all."

And then D came by a few weeks later, another of the neighborhood alum. "I just sat and cried last night, Sister Kownacki. I wish I was little again and could come here every day after school. Those was the best time of my life. The streets are awful, Sister Kownacki. I have no one to talk to except you. No one care about me except you, Sister Kownacki." D is trying his best to fight the pressure of the streets, and miracles do happen, but once again, I put him on a bus to go back to his father in Tennessee knowing he will return to Erie again in spring. He has no GED. He has a baby girl in Buffalo, and when the mother brought her here for a visit this summer, we had to supply food and clothing. "I love you, Sister Kownacki," he said when we hugged goodbye at the bus station.

Though for these two boys it doesn't look like their lives will ever be the focus of a Hallmark movie, I believe they got it right. My interaction with those twenty children for that brief a time was not meant to "save" them in the expected way: high school diplomas for all, college degrees for some, decent jobs, no crime, no drugs, happy families. That would be the epitome of pride and a pitiful reason to get to know another person. We can't "save" anyone, but we can care about them because, well, that's what we're here for. Being human is about filling your treasure box with genuine relationships. I will always care about those children, and I know they hold a tender and meaningful memory of our time together, passing shadows though we be.

I go back to the insightful comment by J, "You know it's a rare thing, Sister Kownacki, that somebody care for you, really care for you, for no reason at all." This I believe.

☙

Literature in Empathy

"I believe in empathy," is how Azar Nafisi begins her essay in the book *This I Believe*. She also believes that we can grow in empathy by reading good literature—stories that teach us more about ourselves and others.

In her essay she uses Huckleberry Finn as an example of empathy, specifically his decision not to turn over to authorities his friend Jim, the runaway slave. Huck has been taught in Sunday School that anyone who frees a slave goes straight to hell, but he looks at Jim and remembers the good times they had together, imagining Jim and he "a-floating along, talking and singing and laughing." He sees Jim as a friend, another human being, not as a slave, and decides, "alright, then, I'll go to hell."

Nafisi, who was expelled from teaching at the University of Tehran for refusing to wear a veil, writes that during that time two male Muslim students came to her defense. Both were members of the powerful Muslim Students Association and had had heated ideological debates with Nafisi in the classroom. When Nafisi ran into one of the students, she thanked him for supporting her, and he replied, "We are not as rigid as you imagine us to be, Professor Nafisi. Remember your own lecture on Huck Finn? Let's just say, he is not the only one who can risk going to hell."

Nafisi's experience is confirmed by a recent scientific study at the New School for Social Research that showed that exposure to literary fiction makes readers more able to detect and understand other people's emotions and motivations. Literary fiction, the study found, makes readers more empathetic—pulp fiction and nonfiction do not have the same results.

Old Monk, who is a former literature teacher and a lifelong reader, jumped with joy when she read about the connection between great fiction and empathy. She even imagined a couple of ways to act on this information. Instead of protesting against injustice in the streets, we should be sending members of Congress short stories by Leo Tolstoy and hosting book discussions. We should be sending heads of state around the world the latest Barbara Kingsolver novel and having virtual conferences to share ideas and insights. What's needed for lasting change is to spark people's imaginations, so they look at the world with new eyes, softer hearts, and greater understanding of the human condition. Come on, people, let's get together and read great novels, short stories, and poems.

Then I read Nafisi's essay again and thought to myself, "Old Monk, be honest, you were surprised by that encounter between Professor Nafisi and the two far-right Muslim students. You didn't expect their response. And why is that?" Well, the answer is obvious. I have stereotyped followers of radical Islam. I must think of them as less than human, incapable of standing in the shoes of a person like Professor Nafisi and choosing a ticket to hell in her defense.

So instead of sending the current person in the White House a copy of *The Adventures of Huckleberry Finn*, along with notes and a discussion guide, I'm going to reread it. Or maybe I'll do both since both of us seem to need to grow in empathy.

Essay writer Azar Nafisi is also the author of the highly acclaimed *Reading Lolita in Tehran*. In that book she chronicled her experience of secretly gathering young female students once a week in the Islamic Republic of Iran to discuss forbidden Western literature. I highly recommend it and guarantee that it will raise your empathy quotient because even though it's nonfiction, it's all about great fiction.

CR

"Real" Monasticism?

Meinrad Craighead, one of the great pioneers of woman-centered religious art, died recently. In 1978, when she was a Benedictine nun in Stanbrook Abbey, England, I interviewed Meinrad for my book *Peace Is Our Calling*. I was asking high-profile people in monastic orders and in the peace movement what the Benedictine motto "Pax" meant to them. Did it have anything to do with building a more just world or was it only about interior peace? Of all the interviews I did, I remember hers the most.

Did we ever go at it! At that time she was convinced that the contemplative life meant cloister and habits and minimal contact with "the world." I, of course, was coming off the heady post-Vatican renewal years and was all about the prophetic dimension of monasticism and the United States bishops' proclamation that "justice is a constitutive element of the gospel." We ended up disagreeing about the monastic life, but really liking each other.

Meinrad left Stanbrook after fourteen years and eventually moved back to the States, continuing her brilliant artistic work in New Mexico. She loves monastic life, she told an interviewer, and only left Stanbrook to be obedient to a new call—to concentrate her work on images of God the Mother. A half dozen books of her art with her accompanying text were published, including *Crow Mother and the Dog God: A Retrospective*. A documentary on her life, *Praying with Images*, was recently completed. And you can still find her early work, mostly woodcuts, where I first saw it, in the *Catholic Worker* newspaper. When I heard she had died, I reread the piece I did about her in my book. Here's a good part of that encounter:

In 1966 Meinrad was awarded a Fulbright Award in printmaking and went to Spain. There she lived like a quasi-hermit at the Benedictine monastery of Montserrat and grappled with a deepening need and desire for a more contemplative life. The way she handled her call speaks volumes about Meinrad's direct, if somewhat unorthodox, approach to life.

"I went to a Dominican priest who was a professor of modern philosophy. I didn't even like the man, but I thought he would be straightforward and objective, not patronizing.

"I made a pact with the Holy Spirit that I would do whatever the priest told me. I didn't want to waste a lot of time shopping around for convents. The priest said, 'Go to Stanbrook.' So I went. If he sent me to a Carmelite convent in the middle of a desert, that's where I'd be."

She brought out the prints of her new book, yet to be published, on tree mythology. Meinrad said she has always had a love affair with trees and remembers spending hours in their branches as a child. At Stanbrook she was in charge of caring for the trees and the garden and spent most of Saturday outdoors. On Sundays, Meinrad devoted hours to reading mythology, poetry, and the sacred writings of Eastern and Western religions. Over the years she collected hundreds of verses, parables, and poems that relate to trees, and these form the text of her book *Sign of the Tree: Meditations in Images and Words*. She shared page after page of charcoal drawings that explored trees, powerful proclamations of a lover's intimacy. Here is someone who knows herself, who knows God.

"People want art because it fills their need for space," she explained. "Because people don't know how to find adequate peace in themselves, they grab physical space. Ultimately this leads to war. Art is one way to get a people to appreciate space. We have so much space already, but we must keep it uncluttered and clean.

"We're too plugged into activity—a transistor in one ear, phone on the other—we never reach interior spaces. To bring about peace we must get people to be in their own emptiness. Now you can only do that if you are there and that requires discipline and silence—and it's very painful. But you must get over the threshold of pain and discover your own space and know the deep presence—even if it's in the most ungodlike sense, quite apart from knowing that's where the one God is. Then and then only can you respect space in other people."

The interview with Meinrad was one of the most difficult I have ever conducted. At least three times I thought she was going to ask me to leave, so at odds were we in our understanding of contemplation, monastic life, community. For a start, she didn't even think I was a bona fide monastic because I'm not cloistered.

Meinrad: You're saying, "What good is monasticism?" The pragmatic American—what's it good for?
Mary Lou: No, I don't look at monastic life that way at all. . . . I wouldn't have joined a monastic order if. . .
Meinrad: But you haven't joined a monastic order.
Mary Lou: Benedictines are a monastic order.
Meinrad: Not in the States.

Somehow, we stuck through the awkward and uncomfortable silences that followed exchanges like this and plowed on. Perhaps a grudging respect built as the minutes ticked slowly away. Whatever, we parted friends. As we were saying good-bye, I mentioned that I was sorry the Dominican priest hadn't told her to go to Erie, Pennsylvania. But she would have none of it—not real monasticism, you know.

Rest in peace, dear Meinrad. And not to worry, I'm not going to ask you what you think *peace* means in this instance.

ॐ

The Pity of War

I did something over the weekend that I never did before—I attended a military exhibition. Travis, one of the boys that Sister

Mary and I helped raise, is an Iraq war veteran, and he brought the national traveling exhibition "Eyes of Freedom" to the Erie Civic Center.

Though I've given most of my adult life to protesting war and preparations for war, I have never judged those who serve in war. When I was studying for a master's degree in peace studies, I read every book that I could find that was written by a former soldier because I wanted to understand what drew them to the military and what they experienced and learned in the midst of battle. What heavy loads they carried home with them in their rucksacks. I learned a lot from those books and remember admiring the heroism I encountered in those pages and also weeping over the personal tragedies and broken dreams of so many. I wondered, too, and still wonder, why the peace movement can't generate the same numbers of people who would be willing to literally lay down their lives for what they believe.

"Eyes of Freedom" honors twenty-two Marines and one Navy Corpsman of Lima Company, 3rd Battalion, 25th Regiment, who were killed in Iraq. Since most of the deceased Marines were from Ohio, it's an Ohio woman artist, Anita Miller, who had a vision of the memorial and felt called to create it. The exhibit is true to its purpose: it's like attending a group wake. In a large, darkened circle, there are eight panels, each with two or three life-sized portraits of the fallen soldiers, most of them in their early twenties when they died. In front of each panel is a lit candle. Each soldier's boots are displayed at the base of each portrait, many of them stuffed with pictures and notes from those who attend the exhibit and are moved to respond. Viewers are silent as they walk from panel to panel, many of them listening to a phone audio that gives a brief biography of the young man's life, his dreams and aspirations, and a touching anecdote, usually told to the artist by the dead Marine's mother or wife or friend or child.

I carried the phone with me and wept at the stories and lives lost too soon. But I also wept because I had a running commentary by Travis who was at the Lima Company dam site and aid station when the wounded and dead arrived. He had to put the remains in body bags and lift the severely wounded from the emergency truck. "I remember holding him," Travis said pointing to one of the portraits. "I remember him because he was so big and heavy." And then a few minutes later, "I don't recognize many of them because their faces were blown away."

"There were one thousand Marines guarding the dam where we were stationed," Travis continued. "One out of twenty of us did not make it home. We were the hardest-hit unit in the Iraq war."

Travis was twenty-one years old when he experienced this. He's thirty-four years old now but still suffering the aftershocks. Which brings me to the most gripping part of the exhibition. In the middle of the circle is a sculptured piece titled "Silent Battle." It is dedicated to all the veterans who didn't die on the battlefield but whose spirits and minds suffered severe wounds. The same artist, Anita Miller, created the piece by listening to the story of a young veteran who was on the verge of suicide. She then sculpted his fears and terrors and anguish and lost hope. You see veterans put their hands on the statue and cry uncontrollably, mothers embrace the young soldier trying to offer comfort, others just stand in silent prayer. In a video that accompanies the exhibition the artist Miller explains that the statue is for many the first step in healing. It tells suffering veterans, their family members, and loved ones, "you are not alone."

"You go to the military for a lot of reasons," Travis said. "Some go for ideals, some go out of a sense of duty and responsibility, some go because they need a job. But once you're there—well, it's war and it's brutal. Only a few, if any, are prepared to deal with what happens to you inside because of it. I know that I wasn't prepared."

Travis said he brought the exhibition to Erie to help others, but it was healing for him, too. "I met so many people who are going through what I'm experiencing," he said. "I could talk to them and now have a network of people to reach out to. I don't feel alone anymore."

World War I poet Wilfrid Owen wrote, "My subject is War, and the pity of War. The Poetry is in the pity." The exhibition "Eyes of Freedom" is also about the subject of war and the pity of war. It is a traveling poem whose poetry is in the pity.

Part Three

HOLD FAST TO BEAUTY

Journal Entries, 2019–2022

❧

Personal Effects

A funny thing happened to me on the way to preparing for my monthly "Writing as a Spiritual Practice" gathering. The poem I selected for reflection and writing prompts, "Personal Effects" by Raymond Byrnes, deals with writing a will. The poem's narrator is told by the lawyer to attach a letter to his will detailing which of his personal effects will go to whom "to prevent/potential discord over artifacts/valued only for their sentiment."

It's a lovely, melancholic poem that reminds us how few meaningful articles we really possess that we would want to pass on to a friend or family member. I mean, does anyone really want my used True Writer ballpoint pen? It also reminds us of the intangible things and experiences that made our lives worthwhile but that we don't really possess and can't pass on to anyone—a first kiss, a shaft of sunlight on an oak desk, the ringing of the neighborhood church bells when my father died.

So, I'm sailing along writing discussion questions and writing prompts, kind of surfing my life in a superficial search for sentimental artifacts and memories.

Then the doctor tells me, "You have a malignant eye tumor. We can either remove your eye or try radiation. This cancer spreads to the lungs and liver, so you will need some tests to see if it has." It kind of shakes you up, if you know what I mean.

I take the tests and they are negative. The cancer has not metastasized. In a week or so I will begin radiation plaque therapy.

Just like that, the poem ceases to be a routine exercise and becomes my heartbeat. I review my discussion questions and writing prompts with both terror and awe. Writing an imaginary will is not so "pretend" anymore. Time, oodles of it, is not a given. Are there any personal artifacts that I would want to pass on? Which ones? Why these? To whom? I look around my room and writing space and office and can't find five things that anyone would want. Even I don't want them. But there are those intangible, precious moments and experiences and memories from my life that I want to try to preserve in someone's heart. No, that I want to relish and treasure in my heart in the days that are to come. Talk about a tough yet wonderful wake-up call.

Here is Byrnes's poem:

Personal Effects

The lawyer told him to write a letter
to accompany the will, to prevent
potential discord over artifacts
valued only for their sentiment.

His wife treasures a watercolor by
her father, grandmama's spoon stirs
their oatmeal every morning. Some
days, he wears his father's favorite tie.

He tries to think of things that
could be tokens of his days:
binoculars that transport
bluebirds through his cataracts

a frayed fishing vest with
pockets full of feathers brightly
tied, the little fly rod he can still
manipulate in forest thickets,

a sharp-tined garden fork,
heft and handle fit for him,
a springy spruce kayak paddle,
a retired leather satchel.

He writes his awkward note,
trying to dispense with grace
some well-worn clutter easily
discarded in another generation.

But what he wishes to bequeath
are items never owned: a Chopin
etude wafting from his wife's piano
on the scent of morning coffee,

seedling peas poking into April,
monarch caterpillars infesting
milkweed leaves, a light brown
doe alert in purple asters

a full moon rising in October,
hunting-hat orange in ebony sky,
sunlit autumn afternoons that flutter
through the heart like falling leaves.

CR

Holy Leisure

Holy leisure is my favorite pillar of Benedictine spirituality. It's probably why I entered the monastery—I wanted to live a life of holy leisure. And that intent is the bedrock of my call, the one that keeps me here.

I consider holy leisure time spent doing stuff that doesn't seem productive. What people might call wasting time: silence, good reading, visiting art galleries, conversation with friends. That's why I so look forward to my annual two-week vacation that spans the end of August and the start of September. Here are some holy leisure moments I experienced:

- Right before vacation started, I was one of about fifty people who participated in the second anniversary of the Silent Peace Walks sponsored by the Erie Benedictines for Peace. It began with a picnic of hot dogs, veggie burgers, snacks, and watermelon in the yard of our old Motherhouse in the center of the city, the area where the founders of the Benedictine Sisters of Erie first settled in 1856. Following an hour of food, drink, and good conversation, the walk began.

- A Silent Peace Walk is just that—a bell rings, the group recites a prayer, you walk in silence for twenty minutes, and end with another prayer. It is not a protest in the traditional sense. We are not railing against anything. The Erie group changes venues monthly. A walk in the downtown park. A walk around the county prison. A walk in the arboretum. Anyone can make the case that Silent Peace Walks are good for nothing. Of course, "what is essential is invisible to the eyes" and maybe walking in mindful silence can bring deeper inner peace. I don't know, but I can't think of a better way to spend twenty minutes.

- Spent forty-five minutes in Aki Himalayan Salt Room today hoping the therapy is healing my lungs, which are getting progressively worse. Cough. Cough. Cough. Day and night. If you've never experienced a salt room, go find one even if you don't have respiratory problems. It's a great excuse to do nothing for almost an hour but bask in the beautiful dim glow of rock lamps, listen to soothing instrumental music, recline in a gravity chair, and breathe micro particles of dry salt. You can even take a nap without guilt.

- Read three good books during the two weeks: *Why Religion? A Personal Story* by Elaine Pagels, *Ten Poems for Difficult Times* by Roger Housden, and *Infinity Net: The Autobiography of Yayoi Kusama.* Anyone rating these would lean to Pagels and Housden as ideal holy leisure books. And they are. Kusama's life would probably be listed on the Catholic Index of Forbidden Books, but it was my favorite. This avant-garde, mentally ill, highly acclaimed Japanese artist has pushed every boundary possible in her "search for the truth that leads to light." Georgia O'Keeffe was very instrumental in encouraging a young Kusama and introducing her to the New York art world. In the book, Kusama says of O'Keeffe, "She possessed a certain genuine and deeply embedded spirituality, and it is largely to this that I attribute her greatness." I feel the same way about Kusama.

- Shopping in Kazoo II is another experience in holy leisure that I look forward to during vacation. We drive to the village of Ellicottville, New York, once a year to spend leisurely time in the store, browsing the unusual art pieces the owner buys from artists across the country, the eclectic selection of "spiritual" books that she displays, the holy images that span traditions, and the unique greeting cards. I always try to purchase something; usually it's a book. I had two in my hand as I got ready to leave and then said to myself, "Books, books, always books. Take one of those art pieces from Santa Fe that you were admiring." So, I did. I'm now looking for a place to hang a modern icon titled "Angel in the Garden" by Christina Miller.

- Though I live only ninety minutes from Buffalo and visit often, I've never been to the city's Botanical Gardens. Until this vacation. What a lovely, leisurely stroll through twelve houses of various plants. House 1 is the Palm Dome. House 2 is Aquatic Gardens. House 4 is Cacti and Succulents. You get the idea. I had two favorites. House 3, Asian Rainforest, felt like a meditation room with its Buddha statues, moon gate, and decorative tea house. I could have camped out for a while. House 8 was Orchids, and what I loved there is that they selected three orchid plants and put an empty frame around each one. It forced you to look at them differently. This morning in church I selected one person from across the aisle and put an invisible frame around his face. Then I looked at him as the work of art that he was.

- How about beef on weck (roast beef on a kummelweck roll), the Number One reason to eat lunch at Schwabl's, a family restaurant in West Seneca, New York, that's been open since 1837? Lo and behold, the menu also advertised fresh hand-grated potato pancakes. Eat slowly, savor every morsel.

- My final holy leisure event was a visit to Frank Lloyd Wright's Graycliff, a Lake Erie summer home the famed architect designed outside of Buffalo. I had toured it about ten years ago when it was under renovation and never forgot it. Now it is completely restored, and what a treasure. The house is all windows and, when you approach it, you can see the lake right through it—no curtains or shutters or darkened windows. It's all light. If I could choose a dream house to live in, Graycliff is it. It was a gift to sit for an hour in the simple elegance of the home and listen to the tour guide tell Wright stories. There are a few sacred places that, following a visit, never have left me. Taizé is one, the market square in Krakow is another. And

Graycliff is a third. When I call them to memory, I fill with light and with soul.

C⅔

Seeing Clearly

Old Monk thanks you for your kind comments and promised prayers. The first half of my eye radiation therapy is completed, and I will return for the second procedure in early November. I have no pain and the reduced and blurred vision (temporary, I hope) has actually helped me to see more clearly all the loving friends and family that surround me. Old Monk hopes to get back to her writing in late November. I've always loved the Antoine de Saint-Exupéry quote from *The Little Prince*, "What is essential, is invisible to the eyes." Now I know the truth of it.

C⅔

Pearl of Great Price

Thank God that Old Monk still has one good eye, and that means she can still read. I still don't know if sight will return in full or in part to my left eye, the one with the cancerous tumor. Loss of eyesight was one of the risks of choosing radiation treatment. Meanwhile, the tumor seems to be shrinking, but I won't know the final result until spring. And, yes, the cancer is aggressive with high odds it will metastasize. But Old Monk has always bucked the odds with gusto and will give this one a rousing effort.

Meanwhile, I've spent the last couple months taking it easy while my eye healed and reading my journals from 1978 to the present. I'd been wanting to do that for the last few years to see if there was anything worth publishing or sending to the Erie Benedictine archives. But there was never time to do it, until unexpectedly there was.

How much I'd forgotten of my life. How much I remembered and could recount moment by moment. There are touching and edgy family encounters. Difficult community stories. Loving and hurtful experiences with friends. A library of inspirational quotes to copy in my commonplace book. The turbulent but exciting Vietnam War years and the explosion of the Catholic peace movement. Interviews with the leading peace figures of the 1970s and 1980s, including a tough disagreement with Dan Berrigan and a later reconciling letter. A handful of book ideas that I never started. New initiatives in the inner city with a preferential option for poetry, beauty, and children. Dozens of books read and commented on. Protests and demonstrations and scathing letters to the editor about some form of injustice and arrests for praying for peace on earth. But most of all—a relentless examination of self and my motives for acting as I did and sometimes still do.

I'm not sure if journal keeping—and mine are all printed and in binders—isn't actually the ultimate ego trip. Like, who really cares what you think about . . . well, just about anything, Mary Lou? On the other hand, I keep going back to words by psychologist and holocaust survivor Victor Frankl that have guided this writing practice. Frankl wrote that there are two ways a person can go through life. One way is to approach our calendar with fear and sadness as each day we tear off another sheet, noting that it grows thinner with each passing day. Another is to tear off the daily sheet, jot down a few personal notes on the back, and file it with the previous years.

Those who keep a record, Frankl tells us, can reflect with pride and joy on all the life they've lived to the full. He writes of the journal keepers:

What does it matter if they notice that they are growing old? What reason do they have to say that they envy a young person—for possibilities, for the future that awaits them? "No thank you," they will say. "Instead of possibilities, I have realities in my past, not only the reality of work done and of love loved, but of suffering suffered. These are the things of which I am most proud."

To hell then with publishing and archives. To come to Frankl's realization is definitely to find a pearl of great price.

CR

The Pandemic Begins

I think of myself as having the vocation of a solitary. For most of my adult life I have risen before dawn and spent two hours in silence and solitude, reading and writing and daydreaming while looking out the window at the rising light. These two hours are the best of the day for me. When illness or travel or circumstances make these impossible, I am a bit bereft.

I like to work alone. Other than golf, which is relatively social, my greatest pleasure is reading and writing—by myself again. I even enjoy golfing by myself, an activity my brother Joe, who is an avid golfer, would never do. "You golf by yourself?" he asked me incredulously, "what's the matter with you?" What's the matter, indeed.

I'm not antisocial, at least not enough to signal someone in the mental-health community. I like people. I prize friendships. I attend gatherings, festivals, dinners. I'm a member of a community. But I find my greatest satisfaction and fulfillment in solitude. The animal I am wildly attracted to is the blue heron gliding alone in an endless sky or sitting by itself, Buddha-like, at the edge of the Lake Erie Bay and then returning each evening to the community, to the colony of nests nestled on the top branches of adjoining trees.

There are a lot of us solitaries out there—some are married or in a relationship, many are single, a good number professed religious vows. All of us fit this definition of a solitary offered by Fenton Johnson: "Solitaries are individuals who, through a combination of temperament, chance, and choice, of discipline, fate, and free will, chose solitude as their means of giving themselves to others."

And speaking of Fenton Johnson, I decided to indulge myself during this pandemic, this time of mandated solitude, by reading his newest book, *At the Center of All Beauty: Solitude and the Creative Life*. What more I can learn and relish about solitude at this stage of my life is beyond me, but still my mouth watered when I came across the new publication. The title of the book stems off a lovely poem, "Autobiographia Literaria," by an obviously "near-the-edge" solitary temperament, the poet Frank O'Hara.

I was going to end with the poem. But then I thought, "Won't most of you read it and say, 'Yippee for you, Old Monk, but what about me? While you gush about solitude, I'm another ilk. I get my sense of purpose and fulfillment from interacting with people. This enforced enclosure is stressful, even agonizing.'"

We can all agree that we are encircled by a sudden and terrible suffering that makes us feel disconnected, sad, and helpless. We grieve the loss of small acts of human contact that we took for granted—visiting a parent in a nursing home, meeting friends for dinner, cheering for the local hockey team in a packed arena. We watch the news and worry about the homeless, the pregnant mothers, the people in countries with minimal health facilities, our retirement savings.

So how do we get through it? Where does the energy to deal with this crisis come from, your energy as well as mine? If my energy to engage the world emerges from solitude, how about yours?

Just two examples of this energy at work:

A friend, whose mother moved in with her to recuperate from a recent operation, wrote me about how they are coping: "My mom says the Rosary every day, I think sometimes three times a day. We play the dice game Farkle together and watch old TV westerns and Andy of Mayberry—it sure takes me back to my childhood. My partner is practicing her Italian, and I am practicing my guitar until my fingertips hurt."

And I just heard my friend Sister Mary on the phone talking about a person who bought dozens of sleeping bags, piled them in his car, and drove through the inner city at dusk dropping them off for the homeless.

Prayer, simple family activities that remind of binding ties, practicing a skill you love but never had enough time for: playing an instrument, learning a language, and, of course, creative acts of random kindness. All of these are sources of energy that will bless you and others.

Bless you enough so that you, like O'Hara, can proclaim—even now, especially now:

> And here I am, the
> center of all beauty!
> Imagine!

CR

The Heart of Things

All the sisters in the community were asked to bring "a memento, gift, quote, prayer, etc. that represents your own monastic life and explain its significance to the group." This invitation was in preparation for a recent Lenten faith sharing at the monastery. Those of us who live in the city, and were following the "stay at home" injunction during the pandemic, joined from a distance.

I brought a quote (surprise!)—one that I often reference—by the Cistercian monk Dom André Louf:

> What is a monk?
> A monk is someone who every day asks:
> "What is a monk?"

I think this insight is the essence of the monastic life, a daily *lectio* and call to *conversatio*, to conversion. If you think you've got the answer to the question, "What is a monk," you are not a monk. I like to play with the question and write my answer for the day. The one I brought to the Lent gathering was this:

> What is a monk?
> A monk
> is someone who in a time of pandemic
> continues to sweep the floor
> mindfully.

My friend Mary announced that she brought herself and a small dish she threw at a pottery retreat decades ago that was filled with ashes from our Ash Wednesday service. "Here I am in body and dust. What I am now, at this moment, best represents—for better or worse—how I am living what I've chosen to live unto death, the monastic life." She always gets to the heart of things.

∞

Moderation

I've never liked the idea of moderation, even though I learned as a novice that it is the hallmark of the Rule of Saint Benedict. It's one of the things that always made me ask myself, "Is your life choice a mistake?" Moderation always reminds me of the passage from Revelation 3:15–16, where God says, "So then, because you are lukewarm, and neither cold nor hot, I will vomit you out of my mouth." When I read the lives of the saints, I choke on the idea of moderation.

When I reflect on the scriptures, I confess before God and the community to the sin of moderation. The Holy Book is filled with extremes. Risking your life like Esther to resist tyranny so others know freedom. Getting so angry at injustice that you overturn tables in the marketplace and lash your whip at a brood of vipers.

Pouring a vial of the most expensive perfume on a weary traveler's feet. Giving away all you have to the poor . . . everything. Smashing swords and missiles into pruning hooks. Turning six thirty-gallon stone jars filled with water into wine. And my all-time favorite—dancing and leaping in the streets with a naked King David before the ark of the covenant. Extremes, all of them.

Then I came upon this quote from Rumi:

> Choosing the middle path
> is always a wise course,
> but knowing the position of the "middle"
> is a matter of perspective.
> Water rushing in a stream
> may only wrap around the camel's knee,
> but the mouse sees the same stream
> as an unfathomable abyss.

It's perspective, then, when it comes to moderation. And what I think are sins of tepidity are my sins only, and no one else's.

ⓒ

Paschal Mystery

Only nature continues to celebrate as if there is no pandemic. The tulips, daffodils, hyacinths arrive on time in the backyard garden. My inner-city street is awash with white blossoms from flowering cherry, crab apple, and pear trees. Nature lives its life when we cannot. And it will continue its cycle long after we are not. Very humbling to realize we are not the center of anything. Pope Francis wonders if the pandemic is nature's way of responding to the ecological crisis, a dramatic way to get our attention for ignoring the destruction we've sown, a way to make us "slow down the rate of production and consumption and to learn to understand and contemplate the natural world." It's true for me.

My brother who is suffering from advanced cancer calls and makes me weep. But not for the reason you'd expect. "Mary Lou," he says, "this pandemic is awful but what it's brought out in people is amazing. I was so down with the political scene and the state of the country, but now I can't believe the goodness of people. So many ordinary people are willing to lay down their lives for another. The human race is beautiful, just beautiful." I listen to him go on and on and I weep. I weep because a good man like this should not leave the earth, not yet.

> It's Easter morning—
> A slice of Polish sweet bread
> Slathered in butter.

I wrote that haiku last Easter. Most of my life this, not chocolate bunnies, was the taste of Easter—waking up in the morning and taking the first bite of homemade *kucha*, sweet bread. This year no sweet bread. No Polish market because of COVID-19. Is it Easter? Thank God I can still taste the poem.

೮३

Beautiful Words

I'm reading a lot during this pandemic and found a gem in the novel *The Weight of Ink* by Rachel Kadish, a 564–pager about two remarkable women—separated by centuries—who, due to being women, suffer at the hands of society but overcome tremendous obstacles to rise to light. The story of the brilliant Ester Velasquez, a Jewish emigrant from Amsterdam who lives in London in the seventeenth century and is permitted to secretly scribe for a rabbi, is interwoven with that of Helen Watt, an ailing manuscript historian who in the early twenty-first century discovers Ester's papers buried in a walled home and struggles to raise her voice from the tomb. I love all this new feminist writing that proves that try as evil and injustice might, it cannot kill the minds and hearts and words of women.

Speaking of feminists, I read an insightful interview with Julia Alvarez on the NPR webpage prior to the publication of her book *Afterlife*. She begins with a line of poetry from William Wordsworth, "A deep distress has humanized my soul." Though Wordsworth wrote that following the death of his brother, Alvarez finds it meaningful for our pandemic time. "This deep distress might humanize us and return us to the good people we are," she said. "I return to those works [of literature], because in a sense, it says to me that this has happened before. We can make it through." She compares literature—written and oral stories, music, dance, all things people take solace in—to a line from a Frost poem: "Here are your waters and your watering place. Drink and be whole again without confusion." Alvarez believes that where we go to find solace in deep distress is our holy grail, the water where we find new life.

I spent two hours today copying into my commonplace book passages and poems from things I've recently read. "Why are you doing this?" I ask myself. Just what is the purpose of a stack of tablets containing copied writings? I used to think it was a good reference source for my own writing or a place I could find a quick inspiration. But I'm looking at it differently lately. I think it's my centering practice, my way of entering the tomb. I know for sure that it is one of the great pleasures of my life—to be in the presence of beautiful words and to hand-copy them as best I can. Maybe I was a monk scribe in a previous life. Today, for example, I copied this W. S. Merwin poem. I know I've already copied it in a previous journal, but I couldn't resist doing it again:

Paula in Late Spring

Let me imagine that we will come again
when we want to and it will be spring
we will be no older than we ever were
the worn griefs will have eased like the early
     cloud
through which the morning slowly comes to
     itself
and the ancient defenses against the dead
will be done with and left to the dead at last
the light will be as it is now in the garden
that we have made here these years together
of our long evenings and astonishment

On Easter Monday I return to a Pittsburgh hospital to get a biopsy. My most recent MRI showed tiny lesions in the liver, the part of the body where my rare eye cancer metastasizes. My friends send notes about how I'm living the paschal mystery in a special way this year, praying that out of suffering comes a miracle of new life. I pray with them, of course. I love living, and if they discovered a pill that guaranteed endless years, I'd gulp it without hesitation. But there is that empty tomb that reminds us relentlessly "dust you are and to dust you shall return." I read a poem once that pointed out that if death were such a great thing, why do gods of every belief claim immortality? Ha!

☙

Journal Entries

During the "stay at home" pandemic I've spent hours reading through journals that date from 1976 to 2020. Here are some random selections and updates as I read.

1984

A woman came to our peace community and said that since her husband's death she has come to realize why we can't experience God's love completely. When you fall in love, she said, it absorbs your every minute. In a sense, it paralyzes you—the lover is all you think about. Can you imagine, she asked, what would happen if we experienced God's love completely? We would probably die from the unbearable ache and sweetness of it. Hmmm, I wonder if that's what does happen at the moment before death: you truly know God's love, it is unbearably beautiful, and then you breathe your last?

Albert Verwey writes: "Melodious rolls the world from God's right hand."

1985

"As a result of the apostles' work, sick people were brought out into the streets on beds and mats so that Peter's shadow might fall across some of them as he went by" (Acts 5:14). I read that to be touched by someone's shadow means to be in contact with the person's soul, the person's essence, and to be influenced by that for better or worse. I could make a list of people whose shadows fell upon me and either healed or damaged. But, when I look back on my life with the word *shadow* in mind, I only travel to one spot.

In the early 1960s, every Sunday afternoon in fall, I would climb the steps to the flat roof of Saint Joseph's Convent in Oil City and watch the sun slowly move across the Allegheny Mountains until all was shadow. For hours I sat and watched the sun flash on wild October leaves or bare November trees, then disappear into the beauty of black. Those long afternoon hours, immersed in lengthening shadows, built a dwelling place in me. If I were to make a movie of my life, I would open and close the film with the sun patiently, and with such beauty, moving across the Allegheny hills.

During a retreat for peacemakers at Kirkridge Retreat Center, one of the leaders in the movement told me how depressed he was because all our efforts seemed futile, the world situation just kept getting worse. He mentioned that he had spent some time with Dan Berrigan the week before, and so I asked, "Is Dan in the same state of soul?" "No," he answered, "Dan is a poet and his center rests in the question: 'Am I loyal to my friends? Am I living my life in such a way so as not to betray my friends?'" There you go. Instead of being tossed in the winds of daily newspaper headlines, only concentrate on being faithful to your friends. Friends like Dorothy Day, Oscar Romero, Ita Ford, Dan Berrigan. That makes for a life of integrity. It's the measuring rod of a life worth living.

⊠

A story from the desert fathers and mothers that is in my top five list is this one:

> Abba Lot went to see Abba Joseph and said: "Abba, as much as I am able, I practice a small rule, a little fasting, some prayer and meditation, and remain quiet, and as much as possible I keep my thoughts clean. What else should I do?" Then the old man stood up and stretched out his hands toward heaven, and his fingers became like ten torches of flame. And he said: "Why not be turned into fire?"

Oh, how I loved that image, equating it with passion and zeal for the work of God, of tossing out all limitations and rules and pious practices and becoming a flame of love. It was all about me and my ideal monastic soul. Then one day my friend Mary stopped me in my tracks with this comment: "Fire is out of control. Maybe being turned into fire means not being in control of our lives." Yikes. Me not in control? I'm going to look for another favorite story to build my life around.

1987

Jesuit theologian Anthony De Mello said that we tend to become like the God we adore. A recent survey of fourteen-hundred Americans indicated that 72 percent think of God as father—6 percent more favoring it than in 1984. Seventy-two percent said they prefer to think of God as master rather than as spouse, and nearly 61 percent would rather regard God as judging than as loving. This, despite the assertion from Jesus's beloved disciple that "God is love and those who abide in love abide in God." It should be no surprise then, if people prefer father, master, and judge, that our world is rife with war, chants for revenge.

℃

One, Two, Breathe

One childhood memory and discipline that serves me well when I am in chaos or turmoil is the time when my father was training me to be a long-distance swimmer. The training process was going to strengthen my lungs, since I suffered from asthma. He took me to Lake Erie and set a goal that I would swim from one designated beach to the other—from Water Works to Stone Jetty is what I remember, true or not. While I swam, he walked by my side, slowly counting aloud, "one, two, breathe . . . one, two, breathe" as I did the Australian crawl as far as my nine-year-old arms could muster. And when I could go no farther, he would swoop me out of the water and carry me back to shore in his strong arms.

It took a month or more, but I finally swam the entire distance, for which I received an extra-large ice cream cone from a Dairy Queen. It must have been an intense, concentrated time because even now when life sets me reeling, yes, even now after I received the news that my biopsy was positive, that the eye melanoma had metastasized to my liver,

> I can still hear you counting calmly
> And feel you walking beside me
> And I know the years have only strengthened
> Your arms.

And I'm grateful to have trained to swim to the next pier even though this lap has no designated goal. It's more like a swim into the deep, "one, two, breathe . . . one, two, breathe."

ഗ്ര

Unwelcome Guest

I'm grateful for my Irish friends, but some of the stuff they tell me spooks me out. Like the one about a bird flying into your window means death is on its way. A couple weeks ago, when the crabapple tree outside my study window was filled with white blossoms, I heard a bird hit my window once, twice, three times until I ran and closed the shade. It happened again the next day when I was preparing my morning coffee. I repeated my ritual believing, I guess, that by drawing the shade I was preventing death from arriving.

When the bird smacked against the window the third day—in the afternoon when I was sitting in my chair and reading—I reached for the blind cord and stopped myself. "Wait a minute, Kownacki, you don't have an ounce of Irish blood. Get a grip." So, I steeled myself and watched the bird hit the window. It was a robin, a female robin. Why would I jump to the conclusion that this potential bringer of life was a harbinger of death? Maybe she was bringing me a message of new life? We gazed at each other for a minute or two, and then she flew away. When she returned, I talked to her a bit, explaining that I was going to close the shade so she wouldn't hurt herself. My friend visited a few more times and then, when the white blossoms disappeared—the blossoms she saw reflected in my window—so did she.

I'm embarrassed to admit the terror I felt when that bird first hit the window. And for no rational reason on earth, except, of course, that death is a little more on my mind these days. It reminded me how often I react in fear because of what I've been taught or told are bad omens, like people of different cultures or religions or nationalities or social standings coming into my life, knocking on my door.

Which brings me to a 2017 *Scarp de' Tenis* magazine interview with Pope Francis that I read recently.

In the interview the pope was asked what he thought about giving alms to street beggars who ask for help. He answered:

> There are many arguments to justify oneself when you do not give alms. "But what, I give money and then he spends it on a glass of wine?" If a glass of wine is the only happiness he has in life, that is fine. Instead, ask yourself what you do secretly. What "happiness" do you seek in private? . . . Help is always right. Certainly, it is not a good thing just to throw a few coins at the poor. The gesture is important, looking them in the eyes and touching their hands. Tossing the money without looking in the eyes, that is not the gesture of a Christian.

I loved the pope's reply for two reasons. First, he unmasks our hypocrisy, our self-righteousness regarding the poor. Why does it upset us so if the person on the street uses our loose change to get a little comfort? Why do we expect such comfort for ourselves and are so mean-spirited when it comes to the poor, depriving them of what little joy they might enjoy? Are you giving a gift or not? Do God's gifts to you come with strings attached? And, the clincher:

Ask yourself, "What do you do secretly? What 'happiness' do you seek in private?" Gotcha!—quit projecting your "secrets" on the poor.

Second, the pope tells us that a Christian doesn't just toss money at the poor and walk on. No, a Christian stops, makes eye contact, touches the beggar's hands, or at least offers a greeting. The idea being that once you make eye contact, you are invited to see the homeless stranger as another human being, someone just like you. With eye contact and a simple "how are you" or "God bless" you are on equal footing.

And who knows, maybe like the robin that changed from bad omen to friend once I looked it in the eye, that which is "frightening" or "strange" or "other" in a human being can be seen in a new light. Those unwelcome guests might even bring messages that surprise.

In addition to reading through all my journals, I'm also organizing all my poems, about five hundred of them. This one reminded me of the pope's words:

> This is a poem about
> the bag lady Rose
> who walks from church
> to church demanding
> five dollars and two rolls of toilet paper,
> to dry her dishes, dust her chairs,
> clean the kitchen floor after
> her fifteen stray cats.
> With the five dollars
> she walks into Wegman's
> like all the wealthy residents
> of South Shore Drive,
> to buy strawberries in December.
> Oh, they taste good to her.

CR

My Brother Joe

It was a Memorial Day like no other. Normally I would have attended my brother Joe's annual picnic. Every year he and my sister-in-law Michele came from California to spend the summer at their cottage, and this holiday picnic for family, and at least a dozen of my friends, began the good times. But not this year.

The pandemic would have reduced the crowd, but COVID-19 is not the reason there was no picnic. You see my brother Joe died last week from cancer. Though he was sick, the death was sudden—less than one day in hospice care. Thank God, he didn't die alone in a hospital room but was with his family in San Diego.

"There is no time like the old time, when you and I were young!" Oliver Wendell Holmes Sr. wrote. I've spent a lot of time since Joe's death thinking about when we were young. Born only eighteen months apart, we spent a lot of time together as children. I could probably write a memoir just about growing up with my three brothers, but this week the memories focused on Joe. The two of us making paper footballs in autumn and spending hours knocking chestnuts down from the trees on our block and storing them in boxes for God knows what. Holding him tightly on the sled as my dad raced us down the street and spun us wildly in circles. He was the marble-game king of the neighborhood in years when marble skill was revered among children. Once my mother got so frustrated with the thousands of marbles that he had won in neighborhood games, marbles that rolled on the floor everywhere and took up precious cupboard space, that she carried the marbles to the front steps and spilled them down the stairs. From everywhere the kids came running, stuffing my brother's hard-earned winnings into pockets and bags until they were gone. I remember standing on the sidewalk wailing aloud for him and his loss. But I should have saved my tears; by the end of the summer he won every marble back.

When I took a year-long leave of absence from the monastery in the 1960s, it was my brother Joe who came to pick me up at the convent in Oil City where I had been teaching and drive me to my parent's home in Erie. My friend Sister Joan Chittister was there when he arrived. "I was prepared to hate him," she has since told me. She didn't want me to leave, of course, and thought Joe would be gloating over my decision and act in a cavalier fashion. Instead, "he was so gentle and kind and loving toward you, walking right up and embracing you and saying, 'it'll be alright, sis.' I was totally unprepared for meeting this kind of sensitive young man and I fell in love with him on the spot," Joan said. Her response was not unusual. Almost every woman he encountered fell in love with him on the spot.

Joe served in the Navy during the Vietnam War. In Erie, I was a leading religious voice against the war, and I was the first local nun arrested protesting it. For a few years I, and the Benedictine sisters, were reviled at local cocktail parties and in headlines and mean-spirited letters to the editor and radio talk shows. My parents were proud and protective of me during that time, but many of my aunts and uncles and cousins were extremely upset and felt I had embarrassed the family. When Joe arrived home on leave, he visited every member of our extended family and told them that I was right. "This war is an awful thing," he explained, "and I'm very proud of what my sister is doing to try and stop it." That's my brother Joe.

My brother Joe was public defender of Erie County for years and, when he moved to California, served as public defender director in a San Diego branch. In other words, he gave his life to fighting the unjust legal system and fighting for those who were its victims. I still meet people in Erie whom he defended over thirty years ago who tell me how hard he worked for them and how respectful he was of their situation. My brother enjoyed driving and singing and golfing and cooking. He was a loving and devoted husband, father, and grandfather.

He motorcycled across the country following his stint in the Navy and after he purchased the Erie home drove solo cross country two to four times a summer, singing aloud with CDs of Luciano Pavarotti, Placido Domingo, or Andrea Bocelli. When my dad died at ninety-three, it was Joe, an avid and low-handicap golfer, who said to me, "Dad would be so happy if you took up golf again," and went out and bought me a set of clubs, jump-starting my golf career at the age of sixty-three.

Joe was a gourmet cook who did all the meal preparations for his family and hosted countless outings that were legendary. I'm talking about organizing huge golf tournaments and then preparing and cooking the dinner for hundreds of participants and family in his backyard. But no matter how large or small the gathering, Joe had the grace of hospitality, of making every person feel welcome. A sister wrote to me after he died, "He was just a wonderful person and always made sure he reached out to make me feel comfortable amongst the crowd."

Joe was a political animal and a die-hard Democrat who didn't waste time with small talk whether he was sitting on a barstool, playing golf with the guys, or attending a party. Wherever Joe was, the subject centered on politics, and he never flinched from a difficult confrontation or conversation. I so admired his courage, how unafraid he was to challenge Trump supporters, union busters, or racial innuendos. It cost him quite a few golf friends and party invitations.

Lots of obituaries say that the deceased was most of all a good mother or father. But believe me when I tell you he was the rarest of fathers. I won't go into a lot of personal matters, but suffice it to say he should be canonized as the patron saint for the unconditional love of fatherhood.

In a Facebook tribute to his uncle, my nephew Justin wrote:

My Uncle Joe was a charming and clever guy who always saw the humor in any situation. In a family of rebels and rabble-rousers, he found a way to walk the line between fitting in and raising hell. Last autumn my Uncle Ed told me that Joe was the helmsman on the *USS Leonard F. Mason* when it picked up Neil Armstrong after his Gemini capsule came down in the middle of the Pacific after an orbital glitch. I never knew that before and it makes me wonder what else we don't know about the forgotten pasts and untold stories of even the closest people in our lives.

Justin's question is worth heeding and I've tried to capture some of the past, the stories, that Joe and I shared, lest they be forgotten or untold.

I had a small group of friends over this afternoon, all of them attendees of Joe and Michele's Memorial Day barbecue. We all shed some tears and raised a toast to this dear man.

I love you, Joe. You are my brother and my oldest friend, a bond that spanned seventy-five years. *Idz z Bogiem* (Go with God).

CR

In the Hospital

A kind of malaise has taken over. I suppose it's my cancer diagnosis and the weekly trips to the cancer hospital in Pittsburgh for my clinical test procedure. The first three overnight stays were not pleasant as far as side effects go, but that has settled down and I am not experiencing any physical pain or discomfort—just some tiredness and inner malaise. And, of course, there's my brother's death. My personal writing has suffered as a result, and I'm not journaling much. I am surprised by the number of notes and cards and gifts and books I've received from friends around the country in response to my illness. People say such nice things to me . . . even the sentiments that sound as if they're already part of a memory service. I know that all of them are heartfelt and they fill me with gratitude and encouragement.

On one of my first trial test appointments in Pittsburgh, one of the nurses said, "Oh, I see you're a sister. I bet you miss not having Sunday mass during this pandemic. I know I do." To which I replied, "Not really. I've prayed publicly so much for sixty years— at one time in my life seven times a day—that I can't say I miss any of it. I'm glad for a little respite." I might have mentioned, too, about not being happy with an all-male priesthood and this pandemic giving us a chance to celebrate differently. She laughed, a bit nervously I thought. On the car ride home, I thought to myself, "Why did you say that, Kownacki? Always giving in to the temptation to shock. You probably gave scandal. You should have just nodded your head and mumbled, 'hmmm.'" There is no doubt that I should pay more heed to Emily Dickinson's advice: "Tell all the truth but tell it slant."

Last week I had the same nurse and when she was inserting my IV, didn't she go right back to our conversation of a month ago. "Remember that Sunday mass conversation we had?" she asked. I nodded yes, dreading what would follow. "Well, our churches have opened up and I went to one last week that was held outside. It was awful. It was Father's Day and all the priest talked about was how men and fathers were the most important things on earth and how everything depended on them. I was furious. I almost walked out. I went home and called my mother and ranted. One thing for sure, I'm never going back there."

Now there was something I could converse about and no longer worry about giving scandal. Ah, I thought to myself, your prior comments didn't shock her, they made her feel safe to talk to you about how she really felt. "And this priest was young and wearing some kind of little hat on his head," she added. So, we had a good talk about clericalism rearing its ugly head in many of the newly ordained and what a Sunday gathering could look like in a church that practiced equality. "If this keeps up, they're going to lose a lot of women, including me," she concluded. To which I just nodded my head and mumbled, "hmmm."

> Lunch
> In the hospital
> waiting for my cancer
> treatment,
> tasting juice dribbling
> from a peach

෯

Eat All Your Favorite Foods

Do you want the good news or the bad news first? I always want the bad news first to get it out of the way so I can enjoy the good news. So, here's the bad news. The clinical test drug that I'm on to try to arrest the growth of the eye cancer that has metastasized to my liver is not working. The good news is that I'm still alive and playing pretty good golf.

They are keeping me on the test drug for another six weeks to see if it reverses itself, but it's a long shot. So, I'm taking baby steps to walk into whatever door opens.

A friend gave me a book by Ram Dass and Mirabai Bush, *Walking Each Other Home: Conversations on Loving and Dying*. I have great affection for Ram Dass—his iconic book, *Be Here Now*, played a pivotal part in my own spiritual outlook. When I opened the book at random, however, I found myself in a short chapter titled, "Giving Up Attachment" and a suggested practice of listing all the foods you love months before you die and then giving them up one at a time. I immediately closed the book.

My spiritual practice is just the opposite—list all your favorite foods months before you die and then eat them whenever you can, preferably with loved ones.

ॐ

Grace at the Cancer Clinic

It's hard to explain grace until you see it in action. I might want to paraphrase what Dostoyevsky said of love and write, "Grace in action is a harsh and dreadful thing compared to grace in dreams." Only the agents of grace that permeate my clinic are the nurses.

I sit in that recliner every week for close to five hours while they test my blood and prepare and infuse my drug and take my vitals over and over again—and I feel aswim in grace. You can find the grace of community here. The nurses know all the patients by name since they see them for treatment on a regular basis. They are genuinely interested in their personal lives and know them intimately enough to ask questions about their children and grandchildren. The nurses spend unhurried, precious time with patients who want to show them recent pictures of a vacation or a family birthday party. They answer all questions patiently and fill the six treatment rooms with healing light.

I was there when a woman in chemo shouted out, "My daughter is pregnant. She just sent me a picture of her sonogram." And the news spread like wildfire, with nurse after nurse coming to look at the smartphone's proof of new life and offer congratulations.

I was there when an elderly woman whispered to the nurse, "I like coming here. It's much better than my nursing home. Here you don't make me feel guilty because I have to call you to go to the bathroom."

I was there when a patient called his best friend on the phone and told him, "I put a shotgun in my car when I got the news about the cancer and drove for days looking for a place to pull the trigger. I can't forget the past, all the stuff I don't want my wife and children to know about me, all the stuff about Vietnam." All I could do was say a silent prayer while the nurse went and held his hand.

I was there when a young father was telling the nurses about a recent family boating vacation and was so excited because he was running a marathon the coming weekend, minutes before the doctor walked in and told him they would have to stop treatment—his liver platelets were soaring. "I have to call my wife," he stammered. "She's shopping at a co-op; she'll be so upset. Can I still run the marathon?" he asked between tears. And then grace, a harsh and dreadful thing in action, took over in the form of a loving nurse who calmed and reassured him.

These instances of grace remind me of an anecdote that I just copied into my commonplace book: In 1895, as Oscar Wilde, the most famous Irish poet and playwright of his day, was being escorted to prison for the crime of homosexuality, paraded through a mob howling, "Shame! Shame!" one man removed his hat and bowed to him. Wilde stopped and said, "This, sir, is a debt I can never repay."

When it comes to the cancer-clinic nurses, I can only echo Wilde, "Your kindness, dear nurses, filled to the brim and overflowing, is a grace I can never repay."

CR

Restful Waters

Near restful waters you lead me, refreshing my
soul. (Ps 23:2)

When I pray this psalm verse, I go to Douglas Lake in Tennessee where I'm on vacation in a cabin in the Smokies. Douglas is more like a river than a lake, but they named it, not me. It's dawn, and I'm on the back deck with a cup of coffee greeting the day. Soon a heron will glide across the lake making a god-awful attempt to chant Lauds. What a nice picture, what a comforting memory. But I think I shortchange myself. Why do I limit restful waters that refresh to my favorite lakes or rivers or creeks? If that's all that gives me serenity and newness, I'm dead meat. How much time do I actually have to spend staring at water? Okay, when I pray this psalm verse, I go to ten-year-old Annabelle, who giggles over a sentence she reads in the book we're discussing together, *Dear Mr. Henshaw* by Beverly Cleary. Annabelle, you refresh and restore my soul. I go to a card I received in the mail from a friend who wanted me to know that she cares about me. I go to an unexpected email from a reader—one click and black-and-white paintings turned to luscious color. Instant after instant, You lead me beside restful waters and there refresh my soul.

I'm a little nervous because all the poems that I'm writing are about death. And I don't think I'm morose or depressed. Maybe it's a good way for my subconscious to deal with it.

> How many nights
> O God
> did I lay awake
> in dread,
> bereft of any
> touch to counter death's
> icy grip,
> or fitfully tossed
> like a shoreless sea
> until I remember the mercy
> given by your poet Jane Kenyon:
> "Let evening come,
> God will not leave us comfortless."

✠

When they sawed down
the eight-story oak tree,
its birthday numbering in the hundreds,
its presence across from the church
built by nickels and dimes from Polish immi-
     grants,
they tore down the sign of
faithfulness of blooming through
war and depression, poverty, prejudice,
white flight, and a changing neighborhood.
They tore down Invincibility.
The church bell still chimes
and pours its old Polish melodies
down the street but no one listens
except for the old monk who lives
nearby and is now
dying, too.

☙

Not Letting Go

Ah, well, I've had to make the decision of my life, literally. My options for ocular melanoma that has metastasized to the liver and failed to respond to the test drug are a risky treatment that injects chemo into my liver or to let nature take its course.

I was convinced that I would opt for the latter and have been preparing for three to six more months on this lovely earth.

People ask me how it is when you know for sure that your time here is limited. Most of the time I don't think about it—I'm still working, playing golf (keep shining, sun), reading, visiting with friends and family, enjoying delicious food. I guess I'm surprised at what does bring on the tears: putting away my summer clothes and knowing I probably won't reach for them next May; flipping through a catalogue and asking myself why I'm even thinking of buying a new golf club; taking a ride around our Lake Erie peninsula and realizing I'll never see the still lagoons draped in October sunlight again. I look around at all the special pictures and mementoes and books in my study and wonder if I should start marking them as final gifts for friends and family. Every morning I wake up and the first thought that flashes through my mind is: Mary Lou, you are dying . . . then the storm-like churning of the stomach. It's the finality of it all. Every instinct in me wants to reach out and say, "no, not yet." Is it hard to let go? You can bet your life on it.

What's there left to read, I wonder? But I purchase a new poetry anthology anyway and am blown away by the first poem, which I copy into my commonplace book. (Why am I still copying beautiful and meaningful words?) Anyway, here's the poem, written by Fernando Pessoa:

To be great, be whole. . . .

To be great, be whole: don't exaggerate
Or leave out any part of you.
Be complete in each thing. Put all you are
Into the least of your acts.
So too in each lake, with its lofty life,
The whole moon shines.

Maybe, subconsciously it was that poem that changed my mind. "Be complete in each thing." Put all you are into your acts. All I know is that when I met with the surgeon at Hillman Cancer Center, I was given a surprise. He was so kind and open and relaxed and self-confident that he left me with no other choice than to say, "Let's try the chemo in the liver thing, come what may."

If all goes well, he tells me, I could be around for a couple more rounds of golf.

CR

One Cup of Tea

Maybe I wrote too much about dying and death because every time I picked up a pen in the past few months it seemed futile. Not that anything dire happened. The surgery they had planned for my liver cancer couldn't be done—blood vessels were too close to my heart—but the doctor went to Plan B and removed all the large tumors there before gluing me back up. Now, it's a matter of targeting with chemo the smaller tumors—two much-simpler procedures. And this hope from the doctor: "I think I can give you at least two more years."

No, nothing dire happened—it's just that once you're looking at the great abyss, does the song of a cuckoo hold real meaning? Once again, a Japanese poet brought me home. Over the years, I've had life resuscitations from Ryōkan and Han-shan and Saigyō. This time it was the haiku master Issa.

If anyone should have equated life with futility, it's Issa—his mother died when he was three, his first wife died, his three children died, his house burned down, his second marriage was unsuccessful, he lived in extreme poverty, and a lot of other things in between. And yet, when I began reading *The Spring of My Life*, his autobiographical sketch that links a bit of narrative to his poems, I wanted to write again. I read in the translator's introduction that Issa's name means "one cup of tea."

I picked up my pen and wrote:

The haiku master's name means
"one cup of tea"
which I sip
with daily delight.

Here are a couple more tries. First, by Issa:

When the farmers discuss
rice fields, each thinks his own
is the very best

And then Old Monk's version:

When monks discuss
prayer, each states
with certainty
that her particular path leads
straight to God's heart.

⚜

Issa writes:

It is New Year's Day
but nothing changed at my
unkempt hermitage.

And Old Monk responds:

It's New Year's Eve
but nothing to celebrate
in this year
of pandemic death—
Wait! The pink winter rose.

ᛟ

Beautiful Body

A poem by Louise Glück, laureate of the 2020 Nobel Prize for Literature, gave me pause. When I think about what I'll miss because of death, I begin to name a favorite place in nature, a loved friend, a special food—all exterior things. But in her poem "Crossroads," Glück reminded me of the most basic and most heart-wrenching loss—my body. She writes:

> My body, now that we will not be traveling
>   together much longer
> I begin to feel a new tenderness toward you,
>   very raw and unfamiliar,
> like what I remember of love when I was
>   young—
> . . . .
> it is not the earth I will miss,
> it is you I will miss.

My own tradition—Christian—has always demeaned or dismissed the body as something to be wary of because of its insatiable desires that torpedo you to hell, or as nonessential, at most a container for the soul. I just finished a Buddhist book that took the same approach to the body—"I am not these eyes and what they see. I am loving awareness. I am not these ears and what they hear. I am loving awareness. I am not this body. I am loving awareness." Okay.

But it's all we have, of course—one body in which we experience what we call "my life." I think of how little time I've given to acknowledging it, reverencing it. And me, an athlete! If anyone should light a candle before the body, it is an athlete. Sometimes when I'm with a group and we're talking about the importance of self-love and self-acceptance, I goof around and begin to kiss my hands and arms saying aloud, "I love myself, I love myself." But it's always a "spirit" myself that I'm kissing. I don't think I was ever really kissing my body.

How fantastic that we just celebrated Christmas when we're reminded that God comes to us in a human body. *Venite adoremus,* "Come, let us adore." And as far as New Year's resolutions go—let's just give this beautiful body one long, passionate kiss.

ભ

Extravagance

I got to hear one of my top three gospel stories twice this week, once on Palm Sunday and again on Monday of Holy Week. It's the story of the woman who bathed Jesus's feet with perfume and is chastised by the apostles because the money used on the nard could have been given to the poor. Jesus, however, sides with the woman. Since the event gets tied in with the passion narrative, the church explains Jesus's approval by saying the woman was prophesying his death and anointing him in advance. That's not why I like the story. In *Reading Jesus: A Writer's Encounter with the Gospel,* Mary Gordon comes closest to explaining my reason in this passage that I copied in my commonplace book a few years ago. Gordon writes:

> "Waste not, want not" was not a sentence written by an artist. And it is as an artist that this story is most important to me. Because in the moment of the washing of the feet, Jesus insists that beauty matters: that the aesthetic can take precedence over the moral. Tormented as I have always been by the vision of myself as Dives stepping over the sore-covered Lazarus

to get, not to a feast, but to my writing desk, I have been comforted and assured by imagining myself the purchaser of nard, the lover with the spreading hair. Because in this story love wins over duty, passion and the body's joys eclipse justice.

Indeed, I love the extravagance, the earthiness, the sensuality, the shout-out for beauty and human pleasure and delight in this brief story. As the poet Jack Gilbert reminds us (and the apostles): "To make injustice the only measure of our attention is to praise the Devil."

ॐ

Aging with Humor

I attended a community meeting recently for sisters seventy-five years of age and older to try to put some concrete ideas around a goal that we had decided on last year: "Provide opportunities for all sisters, especially our elders, to lead meaningful and purposeful lives and contribute to community."

Nuns do stuff like this. We have these meetings and set goals and then have more meetings to make sure we pay some attention to doing what we once said we wanted to do. For the most part it works well, and both the individual sisters and the group get a chance to grow. But, be warned, if meetings are not your thing, you probably don't have a religious vocation. On the other hand, meetings are just what you might need for salvation, especially if you tend to think you have the all the answers. Hmmm, I wonder who I'm talking about.

At this meeting some philosophical ideas about aging surfaced and specific suggestions were offered for the proposed goal. I didn't go to the microphone because I couldn't articulate what I thought was important. Then the next day I read a brief piece titled "On Not 'Beating' Cancer" in Brian Doyle's posthumous collection of essays, *One Long River of Song*. After making the case that cancer is not an opponent that can be defeated, it can only be endured and held at bay, Doyle writes: "The truth is that the greatest victory is to endure with grace and humor, to stay in the game, to achieve humility."

"Gosh," I said to myself, "I hope that I can endure my cancer in this way." Suddenly the seventy-five-plus meeting popped into my head and I thought, "That's it, that's what I wanted to say last night. This beautiful sentence isn't just for those who happen to have cancer; it holds for every human being." So, let me grab an imaginary microphone, pay homage to Doyle, and offer my two cents: "The truth is that the greatest victory in AGING is to endure with grace and humor, to stay in the game, to achieve humility."

As Ryōkan wrote:

> How can we ever lose interest in life?
> Spring has come again
> And cherry blossoms
> Bloom in the mountains.

And as Old Monk reflects:

> How can we ever lose interest in life?
> Rain pelts from dawn to evensong
> And in some deep spot of the earth
> A cucumber smiles.

CR

Dad

I'm writing this from the Hillman Cancer Center where I'm participating in another clinical drug test. The first three weeks of the test call for twenty-four-hour monitoring once the infusion is finished. Prior to that, it's usually four or five hours of blood work, EKGs, more blood work, anti-nausea medicine via an IV, then the hour-long infusion, followed by anti-anxiety medication. So basically, I sit here for thirty plus hours—which gives me a long time to feel sorry myself.

The first week I was sitting in the chair, recalling memories of my father from childhood, and crying a bit. What you have to know about my dad is that in his prime, he was the strongest man on Erie's Eastside and quite an athlete. When he was attending seminary, there was a poem by Al Marusa about his football prowess that appeared in the *Girard Seminary Literary Magazine* titled "Kownacki Scores a Touchdown." The first few stanzas depict him catching the kicked ball on his goal and dodging and zigzagging down the field until:

> From either side the tacklers came,
> They flew, indeed, not ran.
> Like cats they sprang, and it was cruel
> To see them grab their man.
>
> Three on his back, two at his feet—
> All wondered how it could be,
> He still moved on like Sampson strong
> And scored a touchdown—gee!

Yeah, it would take an army to get him down, and even then he might emerge victorious. My dad was a tall, muscular man with massive arms. I mention the arms because I grew up hearing stories about how he carried me night after night as a newborn, singing to me, while I cried. I guess I was a restless baby, and my mother, who suffered from severe asthma, almost died after childbirth and was unable to lift or carry or walk me or my three brothers who followed. I don't consciously remember being carried as a newborn, but I do remember being wrapped in those strong arms as I grew older and he told my brothers and me a daily bedtime story, how we played escape the dungeon and tried our best to force a release from the arms that tightly embraced us . . . and on and on. You get the picture, the image I carry of my dad—wrapped in his arms I always felt safe, protected, secure, and deeply loved.

I was my dad's caretaker during his rendezvous with cancer and grew to love him even more, if that could be possible. As I mentioned before, when my dad died, my brother Joe said, "Mary Lou why don't you go back to playing golf? Dad would love it." (My dad was a golf fanatic.) I didn't need coaxing; I really missed participating in sports after forty-five years of total abstinence. "Yes," I answered immediately. Joe went out and got me a set of golf clubs and I headed out to a nine-hole executive course outside the city. Though I had played golf until I entered the convent at seventeen, I was a pretty miserable player at first. Then, a miracle. On my third time out, I got a hole-in-one. I said to my playing partner, Mary, "That's my dad's doing. No way on earth I should get a hole-in-one. It's his way of thanking me for caring for him."

When I went to the next hole and set my tee, I looked up and coming out of the woods and standing on a small hill facing me was a huge buck. "Oh, my God," I said to Mary, "that's my dad telling me I'm right. He gave me that hole-in-one and he wants me to know that he's still with me." (I figured my dad would reappear as a massive, noble animal, not as a butterfly or a robin or a flower.)

That incident happened sixteen years ago, and it was never repeated though I would brag to some of my friends, "My dad appeared to me as a huge buck."

So here I am in the hospital trying to make peace with terminal cancer, thinking of my dad, soft tears falling down my face, feeling alone and vulnerable, all the while paging through an issue of *The Sun* magazine. I come to the final page and there on the inside of the back cover is a striking photograph of a huge buck coming out of the woods and staring at me. It was a replica of what I saw sixteen years ago. I can't explain the visceral effect it had on me. My tears stopped, and I sat with that photo a long time, reminding myself that I am safe, protected, secure, and deeply loved. "Dad, you're here," I said. And he is.

☙

Storming Heaven

My friend Sister Mary Miller tells me that every time I get a cancer treatment, she puts me in "white light" and imagines the experimental drug as "prayer liquid." I have received dozens and dozens of notes from people across the country telling me that they are naming me in prayer on a daily basis. There is a special cadre of friends praying to Blessed Dorothy Day for a miracle that will advance her canonization process.

My favorite prayers, though, because God hears them in a special way, are the prayers of the poor. My friend, Sister Rosanne Lindal-Hynes, for example, takes a daily walk of three miles through center-city Erie and has done so for decades. In her pockets she carries small gift cards to local downtown eateries. As is her custom, when she meets a person from the food pantry or soup kitchen on the street, she hands them a gift card and tells them to have good breakfast or lunch. But since my diagnosis, she adds this caveat, "All I ask is that you say a special prayer for my good friend, Sister Mary Lou." It's kind of selling indulgences by third party, but I'll take it. So far no one has refused to pray, even though receiving the gift card does not require their consent. That means I have hundreds of Erie's homeless and poor storming heaven on my behalf. And I also have the promise of Psalm 34 that "God hears the cry of the poor."

Mary and Rosanne both tell me that they are often stopped by soup-kitchen guests and asked, "How's Sister Mary Lou doing? I'm still praying for her." So, I'm attributing the fact that I'm still alive—beyond when I should be—to God's special friends who, given the circumstances of their lives, make it almost embarrassing that they are praying for someone as well off as myself.

As for my current condition: my latest MRI and CT scans showed a slight decrease in the two tumors in my liver and a slight increase in the two tumors in my lungs. That is enough good news for me to agree to stay on the trial drug until there is clear evidence that it is not keeping the cancer at bay.

One of the benefits of being sick is that everyone gives you gifts. Really, it's like a cornucopia of kindness. Recently someone put a book of haiku in my mailbox at the monastery—*Listen to Light* by Raymond Roseliep. Did that bring back memories! When I was in my twenties and submitting poetry to various magazines, I received letters of encouragement from Roseliep, who was then poetry editor for *Sisters Today*, a now defunct periodical, connecting me with other magazine editors and urging me to continue to write.

His first letter, dated November 25, 1965, was a gigantic boost to my fragile confidence as a writer. He wrote, "I receive hundreds of poems, but rarely a package as rich as yours. You are a good poet, Sister. I am pleased to accept . . ." I'm not sure I ever really believed him since in the ensuing years I didn't devote much time to poetry, just dabbled in it occasionally. But I saved his letters and only recently—before the book appeared in my mailbox—reread them. When I read the book, I found out that Roseliep wrote nine books of haiku, was widely published in over seventy magazines, and won two national haiku awards. For old times' sake, I decided to have a conversation with him. Here are a couple "chats":

From Roseliep:

> the path
> to and from the rose
> is the same

And from Old Monk:

> the path
> to and from the monastery
> changed direction
> every day
> for sixty years

⳨

Roseliep writes:

> "Old man," I whispered,
> arms around my father:
> no leaf moved.

And Old Monk responds:

> "O mother,"
> I whisper, old photograph
> in hand,
> "did I ever listen
> for your story?"

☞

One of the Thirty-Six Righteous

There is an old Jewish legend that every generation has thirty-six righteous ones on whose piety the fate of the world depends. One of those pillars, Thich Nhat Hanh, died last week.

More than forty years ago I interviewed him at Plum Village in France when I was writing my book *Peace Is Our Calling*. The book, which explored whether the Benedictine motto *Pax* (peace), only pertained to inner peace or had a broader public dimension, contained interviews with leading monastic and peace-movement figures. When I heard the news that this ninety–five–year–old Buddhist spiritual leader, writer, and peace activist had breathed his last, I picked up my book and reread the interview from 1978. Here are some excerpts that I hope describe a "righteous one," and let's pray that somewhere on the globe one has arisen to take his place:

I spent yesterday with Cao Phuong and Thich Nhat Hanh, leaders of the Buddhist Peace Delegation during the Vietnam War, who are still living in exile on a farm in France (Plum Village). Phuong, a former biology professor in Saigon and leader of the Buddhist student peace movement, picked us up at a train station in Troyes.

Following a twenty-minute drive we turned up the narrow, bumpy road and Phuong pointed to the simple farmhouse that she, Nhat Hanh, and others had built. While the war raged on, the Buddhist peace delegation would leave Paris on weekends and come here to renew themselves—meditating, reading, working on the farmhouse, digging in the garden, and getting back in touch with a rhythm and lifestyle that the war had cruelly disrupted. Until they are permitted to return to the land of their birth, the farmhouse serves as home.

"There he is," said Phuong, and I looked toward the tree where she pointed. Nhat Hanh—the poet/monk and militant pacifist feared by so many government officials and army generals—smiled, waved, and took a few last swings on the homemade tire swing.

Soon we were seated on the living room carpet, sipping tea, and I asked Nhat Hanh if he didn't consider the action by Buddhist monks—demonstrating in the streets, organizing massive nonviolent resistance, self-immolation—to be very "unmonastic." There was a long period of silence and then he answered: "Monks are people. You don't expect monks to be non-people. It is very natural. They have to eat and sleep and need to react against war and all bad things."

He continued: "Monastic life is only a means. If the means do not serve, it becomes meaningless. If the sufferings do not shake you violently so that you come awake, you have some false peace which you enjoy in your shell. As long as that shell is not threatened, you do not move out of your shell. Many monasteries in Vietnam felt this way. 'Why go out into the streets?' they asked. 'Our work is our being. Our work is to pray for peace. Why go out and demonstrate? There are activist groups doing that.' Then the war came and shook everything, and they came awake. But it was too late—well, it's never too late—but it was late enough."

That was as direct as Nhat Hanh got during the interview. Most of the questions he answered with stories or riddles. "I think I will call a news conference and give the Nobel Peace Prize to the poplar tree," he laughed. And again, "For a long time I've wanted to hold an international religious conference where people will come and try to take a bath. There must be a technique of taking a bath."

The formal interview was followed by a Vietnamese meal. I was a mess with the chopsticks, dropping more rice and vegetables on the floor than in my mouth. Nhat Hanh finally came to my rescue. "Try these," he said and handed me a fork and spoon. Nhat Hanh kept the dinner conversation going and seemed more relaxed without a tape recorder, his ideas more concrete.

He would give the Peace Prize to the poplar tree, he explained, because it is what it is in the best way possible. "That's all you can expect of anyone," he said. The monk should be the best monk, the father the best father—and in that way one would become a whole person and automatically a person of peace.

How about the international conference on taking a bath? Nhat Hanh laughed softly and said, "We would share with one another how we washed ourselves of our prejudices, viewpoints of life, and allowed ourselves to be open to new realities. Perhaps we would leave the conference emptier than when we arrived."

One writer has said that "perhaps more than any other nonviolent leader, Nhat Hanh has made us aware of the need for a meditative dimension in the peace movement." It is this valuable gift that Nhat Hanh wants to offer. "If I come to the United States, I would come to teach people to meditate," he said. "Once people become awake and begin to experience their own sufferings, they begin to experience the sufferings of others. This is a normal definition of compassion."

Nhat Hanh walked us to the car and presented me with a parting gift. I wasn't surprised to receive another of those two-edged swords. "Have you heard this story," he asked?

Once there was a monk who for thirty years sought enlightenment but could not find it. One day his master said, "Go find some wood for the fire." The monk searched and searched but could find no wood. He returned to the master with empty hands. "There is nothing that can be used for wood?" the master asked. "I found nothing but the Buddha," the monk replied. "Bring me the Buddha," he was told. Then, much to the horror of the monk, the master took an ax and split the Buddha in two, throwing it into the fire. And the monk was enlightened.

"So," said Nhat Hanh, "go home and burn your tapes."

⁂

Hold Fast to Beauty

What to do in times of despair and hopelessness? What to do when a dark night of the soul has descended on the nation? When that same darkness has defeated our spirit?

I often turn to a passage that I copied in my commonplace book from the novel *The Guernsey Literary and Potato Peel Pie Society*, by Mary Ann Shaffer and Annie Barrows. The book tells how a clandestine book club helped the residents of the island of Guernsey deal with the German occupation during World War II. Here's the excerpt:

Do you know what sentence of Shakespeare I admire most? It is "The bright day is done, and we are for the dark." I wish I had known those words the day I watched those German troops land, plane-load after plane-load of them—and come off ships down in the harbor! All I could think of was damn them, damn them, over and over. If I could have thought the words, "the bright day is done, we are for the dark," I'd have been consoled somehow and ready to go out and contend with circumstances—instead of my heart sinking to my shoes.

Another thing I do is listen to Albinoni's *Adagio in G Minor* and think of the "Cellist of Sarajevo," Vedran Smailović. He caught the world's imagination when he risked his life by playing that piece for twenty-two days in the bombed-out square of a downtown Sarajevo marketplace after a mortar round had killed twenty-two people waiting for food there.

It's the mystery of beauty that such difficult words, "the bright day is done, we are for the dark" and such a solemn, almost tragic musical piece, can lift the spirit and bring comfort. Talk about opening the mausoleum door just enough to let in a ray of light.

The church knows all about the power of beauty. Amid the most horrific of human circumstances—betrayal, torture, mutilation, crucifixion, murder—we are given a beautiful story. Once a year the church presents us with the Easter story, awash with angels of light, sweet-scented perfume, an empty tomb, a garden of promise, and the resiliency of the human spirit to overcome any force of evil: "The angel said to the women, 'Do not be afraid, for I know that you are looking for Jesus who was crucified. Come, see the place where they laid him. Now go at once and tell his disciples that he is risen from the dead'" (Mt 28:5–6).

Yes, it's beauty that we must hold fast to. It's beauty—in words, painting, music, nature, and in the stories of scripture—that can transform despair into confidence and helplessness into hope. It's beauty that reveals our common humanity and gives us the courage to roll away the stone and rise anew each day.

CR

Window Gazing

I'm in the hospice program now. My oncologist at UPMC Hillman Cancer Center in Pittsburgh told me there is nothing more they can do for my uveal cancer. I'm still mobile and alert and show no classic cancer signs of "being in the process of dying." But the stamina and energy are waning, and my skin cancer nodules have erupted all over my body, from head to toe. I count at least sixty bumps of various sizes, shapes, and levels of density and texture. These, as far as I know, are not lethal, but they are irritating.

In a sense I feel like I'm already dead. Don't get me wrong. People are very good to me. They visit me, bring me food and gifts, offer to do shopping and cooking, and many more kind acts. It's remarkable how loved I feel. But I can't do much lately except sit in one recliner after another, gulp a few pills at regular intervals, and stay the day. When I do manage to go to a community function or for a ride or a dinner, it's not too pleasurable—lots of aches and pains. I played golf at our Annual Benedictine Sisters Golf Tournament a couple weeks ago, but only managed nine holes. I have to say, though, that was the best time and I kind of look at it as my last hurrah. I'm praying that I get a couple more holes in before the season ends, but if not, the tournament will indeed suffice. I am still able to work but wonder if I haven't already overstayed the welcome.

I also feel that I make people a bit uncomfortable if they invite me out to a restaurant or play. For one thing, conversation is awkward. You can only do small talk so long and weather, clothes, and gossip are something I've never been much good at. If I engage in the latest episode of Mary Lou's strange cancer, that soon gets tiresome, perhaps even scary for the listener. Conversations about the future seem futile, though I plug on. That's why I feel part of me is already buried somewhere. I don't do what the living do, or at least what I was accustomed to do as a member of the living. No doubt it's a strange kind of living. Or not.

So, what do I do these days? One thing that has brought me immeasurable joy is that I have much more time now to stare out of windows. I've always taken a ribbing from my friends for the time I've devoted to window gazing. Now I have all the time in the world to indulge my favorite pastime. And what a gift I've been given. Every morning I pull open the shade of my living-room window, a very large window that looks out into dozens of cosmos that line my patio in the backyard.

It would be enough to watch these pink, purple, and white flowers sway in the breeze and be content for three or four hours. But this month four wild canaries have visited. And what these tiny golden finches do is play with the flowers. They flit in and out of the cosmos, singing a happy tune after munching on tiny seeds. They do it over and over. Every day. And I sit mesmerized, a smile on my face.

Brother David Steindl-Rast has written that "too easily we are inclined to imagine that God created this world for a purpose. We are so caught up in purpose that we would feel more comfortable if God shared our preoccupation with work. But God plays." The example he uses of God's playfulness is a single tree filled with a variety of birds. God, Brother David points out, did not attempt to make a creature that would perfectly achieve the purpose of a bird. What would that purpose be, he wonders? No, our God is a playful God, and when God imagines *bird,* God pops up woodpeckers and robins and hummingbirds and sparrows and crows, no bird made for any purpose except for God to indulge in playfulness.

So maybe that's my final lesson. Maybe I still need to realize that purpose is illusive, that too much of life is preoccupied with "working for a purpose," and that at the end purpose can't be grasped. Maybe my purposeless wild cosmos and canaries get it: We're here for play, for wonder, for awe and mystery.

Afterword

by Sister Joan Chittister

Sister Mary Lou died on January 6, 2023, surrounded by her sisters, family, and friends. The following love letter was written by Sister Joan Chittister to her dear friend and sister of more than sixty years.

There are multiple ways of seeing life:
We can force ourselves to either squint up close or,
far away from the fullness or nothingness around us,
give in to the blurred edges of it,
frown at its sharpness,
simply let it melt into the distance—
barely and without care.
Unimportant. Unnoticed.

In fact, we walk through crowds
and never see them one at a time at all.
We search to see into the faces who pass us by.
But there's no one there now.
We look beyond life's nearest demands
and hang our heads to avoid them.
We look everywhere and feel nothing.

Indeed, we have our ways to ignore life,
life and all its crowding,
death and all its sorrows.

Until love comes.

Then we see every item of life between us—
stretching ourselves to grasp every last iota of it,
numbed from letting go of it.

Or at the same time we touch
every disappointment we remember,
every tear we've ever shed for the want of it.
Every moment of emptiness as it lay closed at our
     feet.

Then we try over and over again
to put all the mosaics of life back together.
Back to when we were not alone
as we are now
or on the way to a list
of hollow days, ended now.

Then, if we're wise we find a book like this one
in order to see the past all over again
with every hope we ever dreamed,
and every word we remember of its insights,
and all the joy and possibility it ever brought
to all our wishes and all the promises we promised
before these times
to celebrate the rest of life.

Most of all, all the memories of yesterday
come rolling in again.
It comes with all its fervors
just when we pride ourselves
for having been so strong in our loneliness,
so accepting in our emptiness,
so new in all our ability to move beyond
what was never meant to be forever.

Then, it's the ongoingness of the past
that lights up our souls again
and brings back to us whatever it was
that brought us this far toward the fullness
of our new and lonely selves.
It enables us to hear the voices
and love the music
so that nothing of the glorious past
can ever really fade.

No doubt about it:
It is in the sounds of the past
that we become one of those who have within us
the beauty, the understanding, the wisdom,
the long, long line of light that now, here, always
stirs within us now, again, always.

Within us new life goes on
but only as we hear both yesterday's past . . .
and accept tomorrow's promise.

Sources

Part I

Mary Lou Kownacki, "Prayer in a Time of Terrorism," originally published by Pax Christi USA. Now available online at monasteriesoftheheart.org. Used by arrangement of the Benedictine Sisters of Erie.

Vow of Nonviolence, Pax Christi USA, reprinted by permission of Pax Christi USA. Information and resources for the Vow of Nonviolence are available at paxchristiusa.org.

Dorothee Sölle, "And I saw a man on 126 street" in *Against the Wind: Memoir of a Radical Christian,* Trans. by Martin and Barbara Rumscheidt. © 1999. Used by permission of Fortress Press, Minneapolis, MN.

Ryōkan, "If someone asks," and "You mustn't suppose," from *Dewdrops on a Lotus Leaf: Zen Poems of Ryōkan*, translated by John Stevens. Copyright © 1993 by John Stevens. Reprinted by arrangement with The Permissions Company, LLC on behalf of Shambhala Publications Inc., Boulder, Colorado, shambhala.com.

Part II

"Snow Geese" by Mary Oliver, reprinted by the permission of The Charlotte Sheedy Literary Agency as agent for the author. Copyright © 2004, 2005, 2017 by Mary Oliver with permission of Bill Reichblum.

Mary Lou Kownacki, "Easter Shouts Live," originally appeared in *The Beauty We Must Hold Fast To: Reflections for Lent 2022,* reprinted by permission of Pax Christi USA and available online at paxchristiusa.org

R. H. Blyth translation of the Japanese poet Issa's haiku, "O Snail, Climb Mount Fuji," was originally published by a Japanese publisher in 1949 and is now in the public domain.

Richard Jones's translation of "Snail, you're my hero" by the Japanese poet Issa is reprinted from *The Obscure Hours: Translations* by Richard Jones (East of Eden Press, 2018).

Part III

Raymond Byrnes, "Personal Effects," originally published in *Waters Deep: A Great Lakes Poetry Anthology*, Split Rock Review Press. Reprinted by permission of Raymond Byrnes.

W. S. Merwin, "To Paula in Late Spring" from *The Shadow of Sirius*. Copyright © 2008 by W. S. Merwin. Reprinted with the permission of The Permissions Company LLC on behalf of Copper Canyon Press, coppercanyonpress.org.

Ricardo Reis (Fernando Pessoa), "Odes" translated by Edouard Roditi. Reprinted by permission of the Estate of Edouard Roditi.

Issa Kobayashi, ["When the farmer's discuss"] and ["It is New Year's Day"] from *Spring of My Life, And Selected Haiku*, translated by Sam Hamill. Copyright © 1997 by Sam Hamill. Reprinted by arrangement with The Permissions Company, LLC on behalf of Shambhala Publications Inc., Boulder, Colorado, shambhala.com.

Ryōkan, "How can we ever lose interest in life?" from *Dewdrops on a Lotus Leaf: Zen Poems of Ryōkan*, translated by John Stevens. Copyright © 1993 by John Stevens. Reprinted by arrangement with The

Permissions Company, LLC on behalf of Shambhala Publications Inc., Boulder, Colorado, shambhala.com.

Raymond Roseliep, haikus: "the path to and from the rose" and "Old man" from the *Listen to Light* collection, published by Alembic Press in 1993. Reprinted with permission from the literary estate of Raymond Roseliep at Loras College Library.